Praise for *The Intuitive Dance*

"Brilliantly written and definitely outside the box, *The Intuitive Dance* is one of the most intriguing books to be written about how to deal with stress and anxiety. Creative, engaging, and delightful in its simplicity, you will never look at your ego the same way again."

—Brenda Michaels, author of *The Gift of Cancer: A Miraculous Journey to Healing* and cohost of *Conscious Talk Radio*

"With *The Intuitive Dance,* Atherton Drenth gives us a tour de force of what it means to be a medical intuitive. I was particularly impressed by her helpful advice on how all people can find their way to an advanced level of intuition. I highly recommend this important book to all spiritual seekers."

—Gary Renard, best-selling author of *The Disappearance of the Universe* trilogy

the
INTUITIVE
DANCE

About the Author

The world is going through a time of immense change and the old ways are no longer being of effective service. Atherton's gift is to help people evolve into their true spiritual inheritance, helping them move beyond the hypnosis of modern culture in order to actualize their highest potential and contribute to humanity. Learning how to master our egos by embracing our intuition is that future destiny.

the
INTUITIVE
DANCE

BUILDING, PROTECTING &
CLEARING YOUR ENERGY

Atherton Drenth

Llewellyn Publications
Woodbury, Minnesota

FIRST EDITION
First Printing, 2016

Cover art: iStockphoto.com/43142984/©millionhope
        iStockphoto.com/12960982/©Borut Trdina
        iStockphoto.com/50383514/©Fuet
Cover design: Ellen Lawson
Editing: Aaron Lawrence
Interior flower: iStockphoto.com/50383514/©Fuet

Llewellyn Publications is a registered trademark of Llewellyn Worldwide Ltd.

Library of Congress Cataloging-in-Publication Data

Names: Drenth, Atherton, author.
Title: The intuitive dance : building, protecting, and clearing your energy /
  by Atherton Drenth.
Description: Woodbury : Llewellyn Worldwide, Ltd, 2016. | "First Edition." |
  Includes bibliographical references and index.
Identifiers: LCCN 2016033140 (print) | LCCN 2016034566 (ebook) | ISBN
  9780738747989 | ISBN 9780738751177 ()
Subjects: LCSH: Psychic ability. | Intuition—Miscellanea. | Parapsychology.
  | Occultism.
Classification: LCC BF1031 .D695 2016 (print) | LCC BF1031 (ebook) | DDC
  131—dc23
LC record available at https://lccn.loc.gov/2016033140

Llewellyn Publications
A Division of Llewellyn Worldwide Ltd.
2143 Wooddale Drive
Woodbury, MN 55125-2989
www.llewellyn.com

Printed in the United States of America

To my mother
for having the courage to show me
how to embrace the intuitive dance

Disclaimer

The material in this book is not intended as a substitute for trained medical or psychological advice. Readers are advised to consult their doctors or other qualified healthcare professionals regarding the treatment of their medical problems. Always consult a medical practitioner or professional therapist. Any use of information in this book is at the reader's discretion and risk. Neither the publisher nor the author take any responsibility for possible consequences from treatment, action, or application of medicine, supplement, herb, or preparation to any person reading or following the information in this book.

Contents

Techniques

Exercises

Gratitudes

Life is filled with synchronicity and divine guidance. It was one of those spontaneous late-night conversations with a dear friend of mine that finally brought it all together. Anne Raymer, who has always been a woman I have admired for her determination and insight, strongly encouraged me to send an e-mail to her literary agent. Working with Lisa Hagan has been a transformative experience. For years I had been giving my clients information on how to deal with that inner knowingness called intuition. With her guidance and advice, I gathered up everything that I had written and taught over the years and created it here. *The Intuitive Dance: Building, Protecting, and Clearing Your Energy* is the result of her belief in me and my work. For this I will always be grateful.

I also wish to extend my gratitude to my husband, Bert, for his ongoing support, encouragement, and endless hours of initial editing. I have also been very blessed to have children and a sister who support what I do. Their stories were an important part of this book. The many experiences we have shared have been an integral part in my personal growth and acceptance of what to do with my intuitive abilities.

The stories that are related here are a gift from many of my clients who eagerly agreed to share their stories. Their personal information has been changed to protect their privacy. Their bravery to face what lies beneath—to find their own inner truth—never ceases to inspire me.

The research study called "Three Simple Things" was developed, administered, and complied in cooperation with two of my colleagues, Roxana Roshon, PhD, and Dr. Michelle Cali, ND. Their wisdom and flexibility to make this happen despite hectic schedules, weddings, funerals, babies, and managing our practices through a major renovation made it all come together like clockwork. It is amazing what teamwork will pull together.

I also wish to thank all the volunteers who participated in our research study, "Three Simple Things." Everyone involved in the study found it to be enlightening and fun. Many of the volunteers reported at the end of the study that learning the techniques was a transformative experience for them. To everyone involved in this study, I extend my deepest gratitude.

One day a new client came into my office, and before we could get started, she told me it was time to write my next book. I laughed out loud. I didn't tell her that I had been waiting for a sign to begin writing another book. Rose Philips, you are too precious for words. I have loved our conversations and appreciated all of your editorial support for the manuscript. You are truly a wise woman of the world. I am privileged to know you.

Along the way I have had the honor of working with some amazing young women who are our hope for the future. Annyse Balkwill and Kathy Bartram-Flood, it is a joy to watch you both grow in your abilities and share your wise woman ways. In particular, I would like to thank Annyse for her time, clarity, and insights that were so enthusiastically offered when I was completing the manuscript for this book.

I also wish to extend my deepest gratitude to Andrea Mathieson for her guidance, wisdom, and generosity in sharing the Vertical Axis with the world. This grounding technique is a true gift to humanity. It is absolutely brilliant in its simplicity and makes living in the world a more graceful transition.

I also wish to extend my deepest gratitude to dear friends and colleagues who have supported and mentored me along the way: Bruce Walton, Larry Steel, Shirley Lynn Martin, Shelley Timoffee, Patricia White, Evelyn McKay, Lori Wilson, Stewart Hope, Russell Mater, Patty Oser, Zrinka Capkun, Judi Bechard, and Elsa Bowman.

To my assistant, Robin Greene, thank you for keeping it all together at the office and taking such good care of me and my clients while I wrote this book.

My work and the assistance I offer to others on their journey to wellness would not be possible without the constant loving support and guidance from the Archangels Michael, Gabriel, Raphael, Ariel, and Mother Mary, our Lord Jesus, and ascended Masters. They are with me in every aspect of my life, which has made my dance with the inner calm a deeply rewarding and precious journey.

Namaste,

Atherton Drenth

November 2015

Author's Note

All of the stories contained in this book are true. However, I have changed the names and identifying details to protect the privacy of my clients. The only exceptions have been with my own story and those of my family, all of whom have given me permission to use their stories. In some instances, general stories from clients have been compiled to protect their privacy.

When discussing God, I have preferred to use the traditional pronoun of "He," for the sake of simplicity. In my experience it is how most people tend to refer to God. This in no way implies that I believe God to be a male who sits up in heaven passing judgment on those of us here on earth. I know and understand God to be all things, both male and female, the All of the All. He is only as Love. If you feel more comfortable with She, Spirit, Universe, Creator, cosmic consciousness, or any other religious deity, please by all means use what is most comfortable for you. It matters neither to him nor to the work offered here.

Introduction

We all strive to create a loving environment for ourselves and our families. We are told that if we follow the rules and go with the flow that life will be peaceful and fulfilling. What if these are all the wrong ingredients for a happy life? What if at some deeper level of our consciousness we know that we have it all wrong?

Everyone, from all walks of life, has experienced stress and anxiety at some point in their lives. There are a lot of books written about how to control our environment in an effort to reduce stress and anxiety. I think we have it all backward. I have been in private practice as a medical intuitive and holistic energy practitioner for over fifteen years. I have learned from experience that the true source of anxiety and stress is the ego. It is the ever-present inner critic always ready to find fault with anything and everything at any given time. I lovingly refer to the critical ego voice as the inner crazy.

If you are a caring and empathic individual who wishes to be of service to others, that internal critic can feel like a trap with no escape. Its beliefs, constructed from a lifetime of expectations that are real or perceived, can leave you feeling worthless, vulnerable, and powerless. I have conducted over 35,000 healing balances with clients from around the world. The vast majority of my practice has been helping people understand how to work with their ego and guide them to find their own inner divine, the still point of Zen. I call it the inner calm.

Over the years I have spent a lot of time thinking about ego and what it means. I was raised in an eclectic household by parents who were spiritual but very hands off when it came to child rearing. As a result, I had to learn how to handle a lot of very stressful situations on my own at a very early age. It took a near-death experience later in life to help me to understand how to deal with stress and anxiety from a healthier perspective. My faith and being tutored in Theosophy, a spiritual philosophy that mentors one into creating a closer alignment with spirituality and the divine in all life, saved me.

There are thousands of opinions on what the ego is and how to manage it. Every person needs to find their own truth regarding it, but I want to share with you what I discovered in my work with over a thousand clients. Maybe it will help you with your journey.

This book isn't about meditation; there are already so many amazing books on that topic. *The Intuitive Dance: Building, Protecting, and Clearing Your Energy* is about learning how to master your ego by utilizing your innate intuitive abilities and finding a way back to inner peace and harmony. Using your intuition to work with ego and reconnect to a state of inner calm is learning how to do the intuitive dance. Using some simple spiritual exercises that only take a few minutes a day, you will discover how quickly these techniques can reduce your stress and anxiety. You may find that they will also help you to restore your self-esteem, self-confidence and, self-respect.

Through my work with clients from around the world, I have discovered that changing that inner dialogue using the spiritual practices contained in this book can reduce stress and anxiety by up to 50 percent. Sound too good to be true? I conducted a research study that proved these results. There are three spiritual exercises in particular that could change your life almost immediately when practiced daily for just a few minutes each day. I call them the Three Simple Things. My clients have reported to me that not only were they stunned at how easy it was to do them but what a dramatic difference it had made to their professional and personal lives.

What are these three simple steps?

1. The most powerful centering and grounding technique you will ever learn—"The Vertical Axis" (Chapter 5)

2. Create deep restorative sleep almost immediately by practicing a simple technique called "Dreamtime Management" (Chapter 6)

3. Cutting energy cords with everyone you have been in touch with on a daily basis using the power of angels (Chapter 11)

If you would like to find out how effective the Three Simple Things are for reducing the stress and anxiety in your life, then turn to "Appendix: A 40-Day Practice Using Three Simple Things" on page 225. There you will also find a self-directed study and survey where you can measure your own results.

In addition to these three very powerful spiritual techniques, you will discover what type of intuitive you are and how to use your particular innate ability more effectively. As you do the dance, you will learn how to create your own personal cloak of privacy and protection, you will discover a more powerful and effective way to do the White Light of Protection, and you will learn how to clear space in your home and office. I will show you how to overcome negative belief systems and fill your life with abundance. I will teach you how to deal with energy tyrants and how to overcome emotional blackmail in effective ways that will help you take back your power and reclaim control of your own destiny. I also share a technique that will show you how to remove the toxic energy that can form when there has been conflict and how to transform it into love and light for the good of all.

As I learned how to use my intuitive abilities, I discovered that it didn't need to be difficult or rigid. I didn't need to perform great rituals or go on month-long retreats or sacrifice my marriage or my job or my relationships. I could have some fun with it. I learned how to dance with the craziness my ego manufactured and embrace the inner calm using my intuition. All of the techniques and exercises contained in this book are ones that I use personally. I have also taught them to clients for years. I never cease to be amazed at how implicitly and completely powerful these spiritual exercises are.

I firmly believe that if everyone understood how simple it is to manage their own inner dialogue, we would be a whole new society in one generation. It would make us better parents, more knowledgeable leaders, and more loving and compassionate human beings.

It is my honor to share these simple and effective techniques with you. It is my hope that you have fun learning how to dance with your intuition so that you can stop battling your ego and find the peace and contentment of your inner calm.

May your intuition help you embrace the inner calm of life always.

Part I
Starting Out

You are not your ego. You think you are. You believe you are but you aren't. That may come as a shock to you, especially when you believe that your ego plays such a huge role in your life. I mean, how do you ignore that little voice in your head that knows you so well?

We will be exploring what the ego is and what it is not. You will learn how to balance the will of the ego with the inner calm of the intuitive mind. You will discover how your spirit development from conception to adulthood has played a very large role in how your ego perceives and manages life's challenges. As you become more acquainted with your intuition, you will learn the etiquette of using your intuition in new ways that are healthy, grounded, and wise. We will also be exploring the role that fear plays in your life and how it holds you back from truly understanding the power of the spiritual divine. Mastering your intuitive abilities will help you to understand how to find the dance between what your ego says is true and what your connection to the divine knows to be true. It is a dance with life that will help you reduce stress and anxiety, which will help to make life more peaceful and loving.

1

The Basics of Ego, Energy, and Intuitive Connection

It is that crazy voice in the back of your mind. It is always there, always nattering away. There are days when it just screams at you, and on other days it's subtle and subdued, whispering a constant stream of sweet insults at you. It cajoles you, humors you, harasses you, and makes you feel like you are the only person in the world who knows how to fix everything. It can also be the voice callously reminding you with a stern coldness of what a failure you are and that you will never get it right. It is always seductive, always believable, and you always react to it because it is your voice clearly talking back to you, and since it is YOUR voice, it must therefore be true.

You Are Not Your Ego

That little voice that constantly talks to you in the back of your mind colors how you do everything in your world. It dictates how you think, how you react, how you feel, and how you respond to other people in your life. It is the true core of stress—the heart of anxiety in my professional opinion.

Welcome to the world of trying to live with your ego.

If our egos create so much anxiety and stress in our lives, maybe we should all be on a mission to figure out how to silence it once and for all. Maybe we should just listen to it because it really is the truth and we are just afraid to face up to it. That's a scary thought!

Over the years I have spent a lot of time thinking about ego and what it means. The vast majority of my practice is helping people understand how to work with their ego. Every person needs to find their own truth regarding it, but I want to share with you what I discovered in my work. Maybe it will help you with your journey. We need our egos. When I realized that, I was quite shocked. Personally, I was tired of the constant diatribe my ego subjected me to, and I was, quite frankly, on a mission to find a way to silence it once and for all. Then one day in meditation I was shown how I was greater than my ego, that I was not my ego, but that I was a soul with an ego expression. That shifted everything I perceived to be the truth.

I felt reassured by that shift in perception when I read *The Dark Side of the Light Chasers* by Debbie Ford, in which she writes, "The pain of our perceived flaws compels us to cover them up. When we deny certain aspects of ourselves, we overcompensate by becoming their opposite. Then we create entire personas to prove to ourselves and to others that we are not that" (87).

I received additional reassurance about how I was feeling about the ego when I attended a course taught by Dr. Kevin S. Millet a few years ago. In his course, a healing modality called "Total Body Modification" (TBM), he said, "We all develop beliefs that we believe are the truth but that they are really the lie. Once you uncover the lie and see the truth, then you can change your mind and that changes your reality, which changes how you live your life."

Once I experienced that shift in perception about my ego self and what it really was, I was able to learn how to work with it and stop fighting it. I began to treat it as an ally that was doing its job of protecting me. I recognized that so much of its personality was derived from beliefs grown from childhood reactions to things I had experienced. My ego just needed help in growing up and learning a different set of beliefs. I needed to allow myself the space to grow and change its attitudes and beliefs.

Much of what our egos put us through causes us a lot of emotional pain. Sometimes that pain creates so much internal suffering that life becomes unbearable. When that little voice in the back of your mind is loud enough, you will do anything to stop the inner pain and torment of what it's saying to you. I have seen it to be the root of addictions in my practice with adult clients.

But then I learned that there will always be suffering—it is one of the Noble Truths taught by the Buddha. We all suffer in one way or another. Whether it is physically, emotionally, mentally, or spiritually, we are still souls having a human experience. This also means that everyone else on the planet at this moment in time is also having the same ego experience that I am having. Everybody has that little inner ego voice ranting crazy untruths at them inside their heads, and they believe what that voice is saying to them, too.

Then I remembered Dr. Millet's statement that much of what our egos believe are the lies we tell ourselves and it really started to sink in. I started to ask myself why I believed certain things that made me so unhappy. I realized that my ego persona had choices. I could choose to identify with what my ego believed was the truth and continue to suffer. That course of action, I realized, would cause me to be swept away by my ego's constant rants of untruths that deep down I feared were truths. I further reasoned that choosing to believe untruths would have me spending the rest of my life running and hiding from it. That had me visualizing a life where all I would want to do was hide away in desperation to save myself any more emotional pain.

If what my ego believes is a lie, then I could choose to learn the middle way and talk to my ego. I could start to ask, "Why do I believe that? Is it really true? Why do I think that belief is true? How is that belief serving me?" As I started to listen to my ego and questioned its beliefs, I started to uncover the core of why I developed those beliefs in the first place. Once I uncovered why I believed something a certain way, I was able to work with my ego and shift its perception into a more loving frame of mind.

I became more conscious of the dance between my ego voice and the inner calm, and I realized that the quiet, calm voice was in fact my intuition. The more I listened to my intuition, the more connected I felt to the inner calm of love, joy, and peacefulness. My mind became quieter. I felt more present and in the moment. I was less reactive, less stressed, and my anxiety levels dropped substantially.

Learning about my intuition helped me find the middle road. The more I paid attention to my intuition, the more I could sense and feel the difference between what I felt internally versus what was happening around me. How the two were different cleared up a lot of my misperceptions.

Feeling Energy

In high school I was the "weird kid." It took me years to realize that other people found me intimidating. Somehow they too understood at a deeper level within themselves that I could sense and feel what they were going through emotionally, and they didn't like it. It made them feel vulnerable and scared. But nobody was saying anything because underneath all those steely smiles everybody was just trying to be polite and ignore it, including me. Deep down I felt embarrassed about what I knew about them and tried to ignore it or pretend it wasn't there. The only way I could do that was to shut it down by isolating myself and retreating to my room to read. It was safer there. I didn't need to explain anything to anybody, and I didn't upset anybody by saying something I shouldn't have. It was much easier to be a loner.

It took forty years and a near-death experience to finally wake up and figure out what was really going on. If I had figured this out in the seventies, maybe life could have been easier, but I really think that I would have been labeled a "nut," to be honest. So I can say quite frankly that I fully accept divine timing on this and accept that I was being divinely guided and protected all at the same time.

Maybe YOU were that kid and were afraid to admit it to anyone. I wish I had a dollar for every time I heard a client say, "I just never fit in. I always felt different." The truth is everybody feels that way, even the popular kid that everybody just loves. Why? The fear, deep down inside everyone, is that we *all* know how to feel other people's energy. I have found this to be one of the major underlying effects of anxiety and stress in my work with clients. Why? The reason is when we start to feel other people's energy our egos have us believing that it is:

A) my fault they feel that way—caused it

B) my fault it happened—created it

C) my job to make them feel better

But the reality is you are feeling their emotions, and it doesn't belong to you. You are not responsible for how they feel or react. That is their choice.

We are all energy. We all have an energy field around us called an aura. We know that auras exist because we can take pictures of them now. We also know for a fact that if an aura gets blocked or jammed up, it will create problems physically, emotionally, mentally, or spiritually. Energy medicine addresses that. An aura is like a great big bubble-like balloon that projects out from our bodies ten to twenty feet. It is egg shaped and radiates everything we feel and think through vibration.

Sometimes the concept of an energy field around the body can be hard to grasp. But remember, even music is vibration too. You can't see music but you can hear it. Your ears are designed to hear vibration. Your eyes are designed to see the physical aspect of things. Your skin is designed to feel the physical and energetic aspect of things. You have a very small organ in your forehead called the pineal gland, and it is designed to see or sense the energetic pattern in things.

Now imagine a room filled with people all with their own aura balloons surrounding their physical bodies. All those auras, all those balloons, are bumping up against each other at the same time.

You are going to feel this either consciously or subconsciously. It may feel like a change in pressure, or you just might sense an energy that you can't quite describe to anyone—you just know you know. It may be that you feel like your "space" is being invaded, but you are not sure why. You may also feel like you know what they are thinking. What it does mean, though, is that energetically your aura is being touched or pressed up against another person's aura and you can feel it.

But can you see it? Let's go back to the image of a person surrounded by an aura or balloon that looks like a soap bubble. It is translucent and constantly changes in color, and it flows around them like mist, but it always stays in the shape of an oval bubble around that person's physical body. Because their bubble is translucent, you can see through their bubble and see their physical body. The same is true for them. They can also see through their translucent bubble and see your physical body. Since you have become so accustomed to looking through the bubble that surrounds you, you have forgotten that it is there. It is invisible to you. It is like looking through a windowpane. When you look through a window long enough, eventually you forget the window is there. Have you ever accidently tried to walk through a clear glass patio door? This bubble is your aura and it is an energetic projection of your inner most being or soul. You just forget that it is there.

Feeling Separate Within the Ocean of Energy

Our soul is made of energy that is connected to all life. Like a drop of water in the ocean, you are a drop of water and a part of the ocean, all at the same time. Everything is connected. Everything you think, feel, and experience is reflected in that energy floating around you. The same goes for everyone else. Your drop of water is having an experience. Their drop of water is having an experience. All the drops of water are having an experience and it creates an ocean of experience.

What would happen if the drop of water didn't believe the ocean existed? This is what your ego tries to do—it tries to convince you that you are just a drop of water and that the ocean doesn't really exist. Even though you are floating around in something and you can feel it, your ego goes to a lot of trouble to keep you from being aware of that ocean.

This is how your ego keeps you feeling separate from the inner calm of the intuitive mind. It makes you believe you are separate and alone. This sense of separation can lead to feelings of being powerless. When you feel powerless, it is easy to get pushed around by the waves of life. It becomes exhausting and stressful and it can lead to a lot of anxiety.

Think about that for a moment. We have it all backward. We are not our egos. The ego is living from a place of fear and denying that there is any love or connection to the Divine. The reality is that you are an individual and part of the whole all at the same time. You are a human being. You are part of the human race. We are all connected.

Yet we believe that we are all disconnected. We have lost sight of how we are all children of the Divine having a human experience. That human experience can be messy, dirty, painful, crazy, funny, joyful, laughable, silly, gentle, profound, genuine or false, happy, or sad. It is all one great big crazy dream that you can change just by getting in touch with your beliefs and changing your mind.

Knowing and understanding this is a truly remarkable gift that will save your sanity.

Let's learn how to dance with your ego and find the inner calm!

Intuition's Power vs. Ego's Fear

You are not your ego. You are a soul with a divine consciousness having a human experience. The pathway to being more aware of that truth comes from acknowledging and embracing the innate ability that you have been born with. It is called your intuition. Intuition is, according to the Oxford Dictionary, "The ability to understand something immediately, without the need for conscious reasoning" (2016). We are all born with intuitive abilities, whether we realize it or not. It is a gift, not a curse, which means that you are not nuts, crazy, or kookoo. Most of us have had our intuitive gifts trained out of us even though we still use it unconsciously. For some of us, we haven't forgotten, but we make the mistake of trying to get people to confirm what we are sensing and feeling. This creates a lot of unnecessary stress and anxiety in our lives. Looking for validation from other people for an intuitive insight that you have isn't necessarily going to happen. Why? Because it makes people uncomfortable. We are afraid to be honest with others and ourselves. I have often found that we are so afraid of upsetting someone else that we will even go so far as to override our gut instincts to the point where we put ourselves or our families at risk. We will even use this as precedent when dealing with authority, which can leave lasting emotional scars. Have you ever made the mistake of not listening to your intuition only to suffer the consequences? I know I have.

When our son was three months old, he developed a chest cold and quickly became quite ill. We had recently moved to a new community and had to find a new doctor, fast. I took our son to the first doctor who said he had an opening. The examination was over before I knew it. As I left the doctor's office, I was worried, confused, and emotionally unsettled with the examination. I didn't understand why the doctor seemed to be more concerned with my son's diaper rash and not his cough and low-grade fever. As I put my son back in the car, I became very aware of the inner conflict between my intuition, which was telling me something was wrong, and my ego, which was yelling at me to "Be good and listen to the doctor. He is the authority, you are just the mother."

When I arrived at the pharmacy to have the prescription filled, I watched as the pharmacist read the prescription. He looked up at me with a puzzled expression and said that he needed to call the doctor for clarification. After a short wait, the pharmacist handed me a bag with three small bottles inside. He looked at me and said very sternly, "Make sure you read the directions and follow them exactly." My stomach lurched as I became filled with even more fear and apprehension.

Despite all of my misgivings and the internal battle raging between my intuition and my ego, I felt that I had no choice but to trust what the doctor said. When we got home, I followed the medication instructions to the letter. Within minutes our son fell asleep. Relieved, I placed him in his crib. As I laid him down, my intuition told me to place him on his side and not his stomach. I felt it was important to prop him up on his side in that position, so I did that too. I put my daughter to bed in her room and went to my bed exhausted, instantly falling into a dead sleep. It had been a grueling day and I was totally spent.

In the middle of the night I suddenly sat straight up in bed and found myself running down the hallway and into my son's room. These were the days before baby monitors. As I entered his room, I was confused. I looked down at him. He was sleeping peacefully on his side. I couldn't understand why I was there. As I leaned over him, watching him sleep, he suddenly arched his back and started to convulse, then he vomited. He was gasping for breath and choking on his own vomit. Shocked and stunned, I immediately picked him up and hung him upside down to clean out his throat. Then, clutching him to my chest, I ran to the bathroom and turned on the hot shower and sat down on the floor. As the hot steam filled the room, I leaned over and sucked out his nose and cleaned out his throat as best I could. As he started to breathe normally, waves of relief poured over me. As I sat there watching him, praying, I was struck by the fact that not once did he wake up. He didn't cry or resist my attempts to suck out his nose or clean out his throat. He was totally limp! In shock, I realized that he was totally sedated. I was horrified and terrified. I sat there for the rest of the night, quietly sobbing, afraid to put him down. I wondered how I knew what to do.

In the early morning hours I called my sister, who is a nurse. After I told her what happened, she did some research and found out that the drugs I had been given hadn't been approved for use with children, let alone babies. "They aren't antibiotics at all," she said. "If these medications are used in combination, they can cause convulsions and vomiting."

My sister was angry with me for giving him the drugs without asking the doctor for clarification. She was angry with the doctor and the pharmacist for not warning me. I felt humiliated and ashamed. She was right. I was trying so hard to be a good little mother and do as I was told. My ego's fears and assumptions overrode the truth of what my gut instincts were trying to tell me. My ego felt shame; my intuition felt relieved I listened.

The whole incident taught me a very vital lesson. It showed me that my intuition was right and that my ego disempowered me by trying to keep me small and afraid. I promised myself then and there that never again would I ever let that happen. I was never going to risk offending another person for the sake of my family's health and safety. That entire incident was a real wake-up call for me to start treating my intuition with more respect, even in a crisis.

Following Intuition vs. Following Ego

I personally think it's important that we validate our intuitive feelings instead of getting caught in making incorrect egocentric assumptions. We do ourselves a serious disservice by not understanding how to read and trust our intuition in any situation. For me, not listening to my intuition in the doctor's office almost cost my son his life. Yet finally listening to my intuition in the middle of the night saved my son's life. It instinctively showed me what to do, how to lay him down, and how to get him breathing normally again.

We all have encountered this at one time or another. Not listening to our intuition can dramatically disrupt and possibly permanently damage relationships. My son could have died. Listening to ego fears versus trusting intuition can also create problems in simple daily interactions, which can lead to a lot of stress and anxiety. How often have you jumped to conclusions and been upset with a friend or family member because of something they said or did only to find out later that your ego had you believing a falsehood all along?

Everyone has a story like that. In the early years of our marriage, my husband, Bert, and I were going through a rough patch. We were struggling financially, and neither of us knew from one week to the next if we would still be employed. Everyone we knew seemed to be losing their jobs. We were scared and angry. Instead of being open and honest with how we were feeling, we said nothing and both withdrew into our own painful silence. Things became increasingly tense at home. One morning it all came to a head as we stood in the kitchen. We weren't yelling, we weren't arguing, we were just having a tense conversation and keeping our voices down because the children were still asleep. Our son, who was three at the time, came into the kitchen and pulled on my top. We were so involved in the conversation we weren't even aware he was there. He looked up at me and asked, "Mommy, are you and Daddy having an argument?" First of all I was stunned he knew the word, that he even had the ability to say it, but I realized it was a moment of truth. I said, "Yes, dear. We are having an argument. It has nothing to do with you. Mommy and Daddy are mad at each other right now. Why don't you go and play?" He just looked at me for a second, smiled, and said okay.

That was an intuitive moment for both me and my son. He knew something was wrong. He could feel it. While we weren't yelling, we were mad at each other. He could feel the anger in the house. He could feel the tension. His intuition was telling him something was very wrong. His little ego could have made that argument all about him. Instead he came to me for validation and that needed to be acknowledged.

I could have lied to him to spare his feelings. I could have brushed it off to spare my feelings. Instead I was honest with him. I was honest about where the anger was coming from and that he was not the cause of it. By being truthful, I acknowledged my pain, and this in turn gave him permission to not take on the pain and make it personal. My intuition was guiding me to be truthful, but my ego was telling me to lie to him to protect him. I chose the path of inner calm and that meant being truthful. It also made me realize that instead of being angry about the possibility of losing our jobs and the house, we needed to be honest with each other. We started talking about our fears and what we would do if we had to declare bankruptcy. We started trusting what our intuition was trying to show us. That simple change in direction toward listening to our fears and addressing them openly instead of making assumptions changed everything for us.

Think about that the next time a loved one asks you if you are feeling all right and you are not. You don't have to give them all the gritty details, but you could be honest with them and say, "Yeah, I am upset right now but it has nothing to do with you. Thanks for asking."

If someone is picking up that something isn't right, their intuition is telling them something is wrong. They can feel it. By being honest with your response back to them, you are validating that they are correct. Honest validation keeps their ego from making it all about them. I think this is especially crucial when dealing with young children, who are naturally very tuned into their natural intuition. It stops people from making incorrect assumptions. Validating what they are feeling helps you to validate your own feelings. Being honest with anyone will help to dramatically reduce unnecessary stress and anxiety.

When I was sixteen, a guy I knew from school dropped by the house late one afternoon in the summer. He had just gotten his license and his parents had bought him a brand-new Ford Mustang as a birthday gift. He asked me to come for a ride. Flattered that he would even ask, I went to get my coat. When I walked out of my bedroom, I was surprised to find my father was standing outside my room. He just stood there in the hallway, looking at me. "Where are you going?" he asked. I told him I was going for a ride with my friend. He just looked at me for a moment and said, "No, you are staying home." I was a little taken back because my father was one of those men who never said no. For a moment I was really mad, but something felt off. I was confused. I didn't know what to do or how to handle the situation. I was afraid of offending this guy and afraid of defying my father. I said, "What do I do?" My father said he would take care of it. He went downstairs and sent the boy away. A few days later my father brought me a copy of the newspaper. He had opened it to one particular story. It was a write up about two young people who had been killed in a car crash on the highway. It was this boy who had offered me the ride and a girlfriend of mine from school. They had both been killed that night he had offered me the ride. I was stunned. My father said nothing. We both understood that it could have been me if my father hadn't stopped me. That moment brought a lot of deep clarity for me.

My father knew instinctively something wasn't right and stopped me from going out. He trusted his instincts and took the risk of making me mad at him. He validated his instincts. He honored his intuition. I could have made a big deal out of this, lashed out, cried, defied him, and hated him: ego. Instead, I validated his feelings and I validated mine. I trusted my father. It didn't feel right to him and I let myself acknowledge that it didn't feel right to me either. There was no ego battle here. We both felt the truth, acknowledged it, and dealt with it. I honored my intuition.

Intuition, Connection, and Separation

You are part of the ocean of life, surrounded by millions of others just like you. This means that not only can you sense your own emotions and feelings, but you can also sense other people's emotions and feelings. You have just learned to tune it out.

Take a moment to think about this. How can you be separate from everything and yet still be a part of everything? It doesn't make sense, does it? However, our egos have us believing it anyway. Understanding and acknowledging our intuition is the connection back to knowing we belong and feeling the love of the Divine. It is where the separate becomes part of the whole. In his book, *A New Earth: Awakening to Your Life's Purpose*, Eckhart Tolle provides us with an eloquent summary of this shift in awareness: "What a liberation to realize that the 'voice in my head' is not who I am. What am I then? The one who sees that" (22).

Here's the thing: We evolve. Our perspectives mature. We learn that changing our minds isn't the end of the world. Well, not for everybody, but for most of us at any rate. Everyone gets lost at some point on the journey of life. When I was a teenager I became lost. As I evolved and matured, I realized that I was lost and started asking for directions. I just didn't realize that I was asking for directions from the wrong things and from the wrong people. I was looking outside of myself—ego, when I should have been looking inside myself—listening to the inner calm voice of my intuition.

How does anyone become separate from the truth that we really are all connected?

Soul Evolution

Before we are born, our souls are in the ocean of love and connectedness. It is blissful, whole, and complete. We are floating in an ocean of love. We are one with God and the universe. We are experiencing oneness with the ALL. At some point a soul will decide that it wants to experience another state of being-ness. It will choose to leave this ocean of love and connection and reincarnate into a separate form. By doing so, the soul is giving itself permission to experience a different state of existence. It chooses to become a drop of water. As that drop of water, it experiences separation in all of its many forms in fear and in love. Eventually the drop of water works its way back to love and connection with the Divine.

Energetically, as our soul becomes more conscious of its physical form, this sense of separation is reinforced by what happens to our energy body (aura) as we grow up and mature. It loses sight of its connection to the Divine. As our ego develops, our soul connection becomes a vague memory of ever being connected to the same source of all life—the Divine or God.

The Stages of Separation

When a soul is conceived it starts off in the ocean of amniotic fluid and is nurtured inside the womb of the mother. The soul leaves the mother's body after birth and becomes its own individual being. This physical birth begins the process of our so-called "proof" for the mother and child that they are "separate" from the Divine.

What happens to our aura as we evolve from the first moment of conception to adulthood and then as we pass over to the other side (death)? There are seven stages to our eventual energy or auric separation from the mother.

Stage One

The first stage is at the moment of conception. We begin to form a human body and energetically develop an aura. We are a separate entity growing inside the mother. Think about that for a minute. We are separate but part of the whole. As an embryo, we cannot survive outside of the mother. We are intimately connected to the mother through an umbilical cord that feeds and nurtures us.

Stage Two

The second stage of separation occurs at birth. A child, now outside of the mother's body, is totally reliant on the mother and father. Its only form of communication with the world around it is through movement and crying. A newborn is intuition in its purest state. It knows when it is hungry, tired, in pain, hot, cold, or scared. It only knows "itself" and how it feels. A mother who is in touch with her intuition will soon find herself able to "read" her baby's needs intuitively. We see this intuitive behavior with contented babies. They don't need to cry out to get their needs met. Their in-tune parent trusts their intuitive sense. Mutual intuition will eventually result in a form of internal sign language felt and understood between both parent and child. Soon all that is needed is a look or a gesture. Most mothers will often comment that "I always seem to wake up about two seconds before the baby cries," or "I just knew something didn't feel right and called the doctor."

Stage Three

The third stage of separation from the Divine happens around the age of two. This is the advent of the terrible twos, when the toddler begins to speak and voice his or her needs. The intuitive parent understands and feels the separation. They realize that this is the first real step into independence, and parents will work with the child to help them develop the first rudimentary socialization skills necessary for survival in their community. A parent who is fearful will fight the separation and try to keep the baby from growing up too fast. They don't understand that on the one hand, the child is afraid of its own separation, and on the other hand, it needs to begin to separate. The process of energetic separation from the mother's energy field is necessary in order for the child to develop trust in its own intuitive senses.

We create a double standard when we trust that a baby has to fall in order to learn how to walk but we won't trust that a toddler knows when it is full and can't eat any more food. On one hand we nurture instinct—learning how to walk, yet we take it away on the other hand—forcing a child to finish its supper when they are feeling full or unwell.

Stage Four

The fourth stage of energetic separation between a parent and child is around the age of five. In Western society, this is when we send the child off to school. Suddenly the child is in a room with a whole bunch of other little beings running around. This is when the five-year-old begins to realize that not only are they separate from their parents but there are all these other little beings who are also separate. Being with other small children at this stage creates a huge shift in emotional perspective and intuitive senses. All of sudden these little souls are faced with major decisions that have to be made without insight or guidance from a parent. Who are they supposed to listen to, teachers or parents? How are they supposed to respond to other children who are also telling them what to do? What do they do if they don't want to play that game because it doesn't feel right?

For a child who has not had much contact with other small children, the first day of kindergarten can be traumatic. As a result, they can begin to develop irrational fears because they are unprepared for the physical change.

If a child at this stage in their life is not allowed to express their feelings or be in touch with their intuition, this transition can create a deep sense of isolation and separation. With that sense of separation comes fear. The five-year-old is moving out into the world. They live at home and they live at school.

Five-year-olds can be deeply and emotionally influenced by fear as they feel their way and learn how to live with the outside world. Parents begin to say, "Be careful crossing the street," "Don't talk to strangers!" "Stay close to Mom and Dad." Yet what do they see? Mom and Dad crossing the street; Mom and Dad talking to the strange lady at the grocery store; Mom and Dad leaving in separate cars to go to separate places. How is a child supposed to respond to that? We say one thing but then do another.

A five-year-old has difficulty understanding the difference. They see and hear one thing but intuitively perceive another. They are still very connected energetically to the mother. They can feel her instinctively, yet she does things and says things that the five-year-old is not allowed to do.

Every new experience reinforces that they are separate. Little things become their physical reality. "I have to go to bed at seven but Mom and Dad can do what they want." And we wonder why little kids fight their bedtimes. My three-year-old daughter taught me that little lesson.

Children from birth to age five are undergoing the most dramatic energetic development and changes of their life. They have little to no emotional context for understanding what is happening to them. They only know that they are becoming more competent at doing more for themselves. As a result, they need and crave routine and structure in their lives because it is their safety net.

The wise parent isn't afraid to embrace a small child's need for loving guidance, structure, and a regular routine. These are children who will be much more content and will do well in school because they know there is someone there to guide them through their ego development and energetic separation.

Stage Five

By the age of eight, we enter the fifth stage of separation between a mother and her child. At this age, give or take a year or so, an eight-year-old starts to realize that they are totally separate from the parents and can exist without any assistance from them. I vividly remember this phase of separation for me when I was that age. I came home from school and looked at my mom and realized that I could take care of myself. I didn't need her anymore. I could survive on my own. I knew how to make a sandwich, go to school, do my homework, and put myself to bed.

I sat down next to my mother, who was an artist, and watched her work on one of her paintings at the time and asked her, "When you die, who gets the artwork?" My mother, who was a Theosophist, just laughed and said, "Oh, look, you are growing up. Good for you. You can share them with your sister." She turned back to her painting and I left the room feeling quite pleased with myself. Years later I realized how much that simple exchange with my mother acknowledged my intuition. She recognized that I felt separate from her and she let me know that it was okay and perfectly normal. She accepted this stage of my soul development. She understood that I needed confirmation and she affirmed that. It was okay for both of us to trust the process. I know that back then I had left the room feeling loved and acknowledged.

Stage Six

The next major stage of soul separation is called the sixth separation. It usually occurs around the age of thirteen—the dreaded puberty years. Energetically, in Theosophical terms, this is the big one. This is when the child begins the largest separation from the mother's energy field. This is when teenagers begin to form their own totally independent energy field. As they begin to physically and emotionally mature, their chakra systems will undergo a major transition as well.

This is the period of internal angst when you try to figure out who you are in the grand scheme of life. We all remember that, don't we? You feel totally isolated and scared. For most of us, this is when we begin to really believe the ego's silly rants and posturing, even though it makes us feel totally disconnected and misunderstood by everyone. This is when we feel the most unloved and isolated because we have totally lost touch with the inner calm of the divine that helps us to feel loved and nurtured.

Stage Seven

The final separation is called the seventh separation, and it happens around the age of twenty-one. It is the final step into your own energy field of your own making. For most people, this is when they leave home or graduate from college. They are their own person. They follow their own counsel, pay their own bills, fall in love, and go to work. Between the ages of eighteen to twenty-five, we do most of our own private soul maturation. If we are fully entrenched and believe whatever our ego has created to be true, it can be gut wrenching and debilitating.

Final Separation

If any of these stages of energetic separation is interfered with in any way by a parent, a traumatic life event, illness, or community belief systems, the child can develop irrational fears or become emotionally stagnated. It can lay the ground work for a lifetime of negative beliefs that can cause stress and anxiety, addictions, phobias, or depression. It can also be a rich time of soul development that can result in highly tuned intuition and/or spiritual advancement. During each of these stages of separation, we are either honing or interfering with our sense of separation or connection. It is no wonder so many of us end up in therapy.

Changing Your Experience through Intuition

You chose to have a separate experience. Understanding how you became separate in the first place is an important part of the journey. We are hardwired to this physical and spiritual experience; how you handle the transition is not. You can change the experience and make it easier using your intuition to reconnect to your inner calm. Separation feeds your ego and learning that is a part of the journey. The fact that you can choose how to deal with the ego is the interesting part. The more you learn about it and how to choose to shepherd yourself through this shift in soul consciousness will help you to reduce the anxiety and stress in your life. That is why you are reading this right now, because you are ready to start using your intuitive abilities. Congratulations! Welcome to the fun bits!

The journey now is to help you get back in touch with your intuition so that you can experience the inner calm as a natural part of your day. It won't stop the ego, but it sure will teach you how to turn down the noise and make it sound like a music track playing in the background. You can choose to tune in or tune out. It is your choice.

Intuition

Over the years I have found that there is a little trick to developing your intuition. But before I share that with you, I would like to caution you about creating any expectations of how you think it should be. If we expect to learn something a certain way, it will create roadblocks to how we learn it. If we are stubborn enough, it will prevent us from actually learning something different. Concrete thoughts and beliefs are hard to shift. Just ask Galileo when he tried to tell the Church the Earth moved around the sun. We laugh now, but the Church was not amused. The Church had certain expectations on how things should be. They felt threatened when the status quo was challenged. We too have had our moments when we refused to shift our perceptions and beliefs about something.

When I was a teenager, I was on a mission to see auras. Don't ask me why, I thought it would be cool, I guess. Before I started to learn about them, however, I believed that you had to be born with the ability to "see" an aura. If you didn't see them naturally, then you were not supposed to. Then I found out you could train yourself to see an aura. I was giddy with excitement. I promptly purchased every book that promised to teach you how to do it. Everything I read, though, taught you how to see an aura using your physical eyes. As hard as I tried and as much as I practiced, I couldn't see an aura with my physical eyes. All I received for the effort was a headache and my ego voice telling me I was nuts or lazy. I gave up in disgust. What I didn't realize at the time was that I had been stymied by my own expectations about how one was supposed to "see" them. Once I let go of my expectations, I understood that.

What was the trick?

The trick was finding out what type of intuitive I was. How I "saw" an aura was different. I can't see them with my physical eyes, but I do "see" them with my mind's eye or third eye because I am a clairvoyant intuitive. I never knew that there were different ways to "see" an aura. I didn't know that there were different ways to use one's intuition. Once I started to focus on my clairvoyant ability, I found I could manage my intuition more effectively. The more I practiced using my intuition as a clairvoyant, the easier life became. I wasn't so anxious all the time.

In order to be connected to the inner calm and reduce my anxiety and stress, I had to understand my intuition from a different point of view. When I stopped expecting things to happen in a certain way, I was able to not only "see" auras but I was able to develop a deeper connection to my intuition. Accepting how I knew what I knew helped me to dramatically reduce how I reacted to the world. It showed me that there was a difference between the inner crazy my ego created and the inner calm that my intuition offered.

Recognizing how I was intuitive was the first step. Understanding that there were different types of intuition was the next step. Life just became a whole lot more logical. I realized that I was perfectly normal and my intuition was opening a door to a deeper level of spirituality that I thought would only come if I joined a monastery somewhere.

For the first time I could see how my intuition was helping me bridge the understanding of how I was part of the greater whole. I felt more connected and at peace.

2

The Four Forms of Intuition

Learning how to use your intuition is a whole new way of dancing around your ego and enjoying the sense of peace that comes from being in touch with your own inner calm. As you master this inborn talent, you may be surprised at how quickly it becomes second nature. Your intuitive ability to make wiser and healthier choices for you and your family will surprise you and enrich your life in ways you never thought possible. Recognizing your own intuitive abilities will also help you to encourage your children to use and understand their own natural intuitive abilities as well.

How do we know that intuition is a natural part of who we are? It is simple. Mothers, for example, are innately connected to their children. Most mothers seem to have "eyes in the back of their heads." How often did your mother seem to know when you were up to something naughty? If you are a parent, how often have you known something seemed wrong with your child only to find out that you were right?

The stockbroker on Bay Street may be described as having "good instincts" for business deals or stocks. The administrative assistant who really "knows" her boss is able to stay two steps ahead of her at any given time. Couples with strong marriages will often be described as "being like two old shoes," and they are known for finishing each other's sentences. The Myers-Briggs personality assessment even uses intuitiveness as one of their markers. This is how predominant this characteristic exhibits itself—not only in the real world but in business as well.

Instincts, hunches, insights, innate wisdom—these are all words that define the same basic ability—intuition. How do you know for sure if you have it? I will show you how. It may surprise you to learn that you were actually born with it. It is coded into your genetic make-up. Remember the definition of intuition is the "ability to understand something immediately, without the need for conscious reasoning."

We all have that natural ability to know when something doesn't feel right or have a sense that something is just off. Everyone says it at one time or another. Chances are you already have a story where something in your life didn't feel right and you acted on it. Maybe it's your ability to walk into a meeting and get a feel for the room and know how to close the deal. Maybe you remember attending a family Christmas party and you had a feeling a relative wasn't doing very well, only to find out later that you were correct in your impressions. Yes, you can argue with any of these scenarios logically and say it was because you could read their body language. However, we forget energy travels faster than light. This means that we can feel first. Feelings create energy waves that we can sense intuitively. We then react physically based on what we are already sensing. Their body language only confirms visually what you are already feeling about them.

We are all energy. We are physical matter and energy waves all at the same time. Think of an atom with electrons and protons. Einstein recognized that energy and matter are one and the same thing when he developed the equation $E=mc^2$, thereby proving that matter can exist both as a solid and as energy at the same time. The human body is made up of matter and energy. The energy pattern that emanates from all living things, including the human body, has an energy signature. We call it an aura. Intuitively, we all see auras and can sense them.

We have lost this natural ability due to society's overall accepted belief that they do not exist. Especially when scientists have declared that they do not exist because they have been unable to prove their existence. This shuts down what we know to be true for us. We want to fit in and not be seen confronting "rational" thought.

Yet, we now know that auras exist because we can photograph them using various techniques such as Kirlian photography and gas distribution visualization (GDV) techniques. When scientists began to study the auric patterns they were seeing using these methods, they discovered that they could predict how and when a person would get sick—something that healers and shamans, who are highly intuitive, have known for thousands of years.

Being able to see an aura with your physical eyes is not necessary in order to read them. You also don't need to see auras in order to sense and feel what is happening around you physically or emotionally. You can read a person's energy field by learning how to listen to your intuition. You only need to give yourself the permission to trust what you are feeling or sensing. When you do, we call it "using your intuition."

Reclaiming Your Intuition

How do you allow yourself to remember your natural intuitive abilities? It is easier than you think. I was totally unaware that what I felt about people was called intuition. Why? Because no one had ever told me that what I was doing had a name. I just thought everybody did "it." My hope is that by helping you to identify "it" that you will discover that you too have had "it" all along. You just need to give yourself permission to remember and then learn how to use it more consciously. If you do give yourself that permission, you will find how much more peaceful life becomes. Eventually you will feel the inner calm in stressful situations. You will begin to see that everything that is going on around you is not all about you. This will give you the space you need to process your own feelings and not get caught up in another person's drama.

If someone had told me twenty years ago that I would be using my intuition to help others on their healing journey, I would have laughed myself to tears. It took me a long time to recognize what it was. It didn't happen overnight for me. I didn't recognize just how intuitive I was until I was in my early thirties. It was a shock to me to be told there was a name for what I did. I was even more surprised when I learned that I could develop it and help other people. I went from being a medical technologist to office manager to training as a medical intuitive. Today I have a very busy private practice with an international client base. The mystery of life!

Becoming aware of my intuitive ability happened quite by accident. In the early 1980s I was working as a registered medical technologist. My industry at this time was undergoing radical changes in automation, which resulted in downsizing in a large majority of laboratories. At one point during this transition it was predicted that over 50 percent of medical technologists would find their careers obsolete over the next ten years. The private laboratory I worked for at the time had notified us that it was getting ready for some major layoffs. Everyone was affected. To their credit, the owners of the lab asked, "What was going to happen to all these people who were being laid off and what can we do to help them?"

It was decided by upper management that the best course of action was to try and help us discover what our skill sets were. They arranged to have a team of training consultants come into the lab for a two-day workshop. It was explained to us that this team of experts would help us analyze our personal skill sets through various testing techniques, including an analysis of personality traits. By understanding our skill set, we were told it would give us a better chance of applying those skills in other fields of employment. It was an intense two days but one of the best things I was ever able to do. It helped the large majority of us who worked at that lab to find gainful employment in new fields afterward.

During the workshop, all of the tests consistently identified me as being very intuitive. That was a surprise. Back then I didn't really understand what it meant to be "an intuitive." For me, listening to that inner calm was like breathing. It was just something I did without thinking. I was discovering something new about myself. Boy, did that little piece of information eventually have a huge impact on my life!

Finding out that there were four different types of intuition helped me to zone into my particular intuitive skill set, which helped me to be more accurate. Everyone has all four, but one will tend to be more dominant than the others. Once I understood what my dominant type of intuition was, it made it so much easier to focus on that strength and develop it. The more I practiced, the more comfortable I became with trusting the information I was receiving. I also quickly learned that how

I read something intuitively is not how my colleagues read things intuitively. This taught me that everyone was different when it came to how they use their own innate intuitive gift, and that was okay.

The first step to understanding how to use your intuition is to figure out what your dominant intuition type is. Once you know, the rest is easy; all you have to do is practice. With regular practice, you will find it easier to trust what you are sensing and feeling intuitively. Over time you will begin to notice that you are much calmer, less reactive, and more present. People will begin to comment that you have changed somehow and they can't quite put their finger on it. It is my hope that as you discover more about your intuition, life will become more calm and peaceful for you. After I had been practicing and using my intuition more consciously on a daily basis, my kids told me I seemed happier. That made me smile.

To find out what type of intuitive you are, we need to first take a look at what the different types of intuition are and what they mean. Then we will take you through a quick little quiz that will help you identify what type of intuitive you are.

Identifying Your Intuitive Type

The four different types of intuition are: clairvoyance, clairsentience, clairaudience and claircognizance.

Clairvoyance

Clairvoyance is called "clear seeing." It is the form of intuition that utilizes one's ability to see things inside the mind as pictures, images, short movies, symbols, or as impressions. It is considered the most symbolic of all the intuitive abilities.

Clairvoyance utilizes a chakra in the forehead called the sixth chakra. This chakra is also referred to as the third eye in ancient Hindu texts. *Chakra* is the Sanskrit word for "wheel" and signifies one of seven basic energy centers in the body. Each one of these centers correlates to a major nerve ganglia that branches forth from the spinal column. Each chakra is related to physical and emotional components in the body and aura.

The third eye chakra perceives subtle energy patterns and wave-lengths and translates this information into clear pictures or impressions. These images can appear on an imaginary screen in your mind in the form of movies, colors, or symbols, and they can be holographic in nature. In essence, the images act like your own internal movie projector. These images or movies can be in color or black and white. They can also be quick impressions that create a visual in your mind's eye. It is quite common for people who are predominately clairvoyant to have very vivid dreams.

For me, images pop up like they are floating to the surface of a screen. Do you remember the magic eight balls that were all the rage back in the 1970s? You would ask the ball a question, shake the ball, and then turn it upside down to see what answer floats to the top of the window. Images coming to the surface are like that for me when I am seeing something clairvoyantly. I also have had times when I see images that string together like a slide show. For others, the image can fade in or out like a presentation on a movie screen. One friend of mine refers to her clairvoyant images as being like flash cards. If I am working with a client and there is a past life connection, a movie screen will sometimes open up in my mind's eye and play. Once I have relayed the information to the client, the movie screen will fade to black.

A simple example of how something would appear to a clairvoyant starts with someone asking if you would like an orange. If you are a clairvoyant, you will first "see" an orange flash in your mind's eye before deciding if you would like to have one to eat.

Clairsentience

Clairsentience is called "clear feeling." It is the form of intuition that utilizes one's ability to feel or physically sense information in their body. Clairsentients receive most of their intuitive information as feelings through the third chakra, called the solar plexus located just above the belly button. People who are predominantly clairsentient will often talk about how they have "gut reactions" to events or situations. A clairsentient can also "feel" information anywhere in their bodies, and this is called having a "body clue." For example, if a clairsentient is talking to someone who has a sore elbow, their elbow will start to feel sore as well.

They are the most sensitive of all the intuitives because of their ability to feel other people's emotions. While they are the most truly empathic and compassionate of all the intuitive abilities, it does create a bit of a conundrum for them. They are considered to be little human Velcros because they pick up everything going on around them. This often creates a lot of confusion because they lose touch with what they are feeling physically and emotionally versus what another is feeling physically or emotionally. They get lost in the noise and can be easily overwhelmed as a result.

I have colleagues who are extremely clairsentient. They always know what is wrong with a client by what they feel in their own body. If a client has a knee problem, then their knee aches. If a client has a headache, they feel a headache in their own body. Some clairsentients can also have an intuitive read on something through smells and taste. These types of clairsentients can be very sensitive to scents and can be picky eaters. One young woman I worked with years ago couldn't eat meat because she could taste the emotional trauma of the animal in her body. Eating the meat always made her feel emotionally ill afterward.

Again, asking a clairsentient if they would like to have an orange can be a simple indicator. Clairsentients will have a sense of what it feels like, tastes like, or smells like. They will then check in to see if they feel hungry.

Clairaudience

Clairaudience is called "clear hearing." It is the form of intuition that utilizes one's ability to hear information inside their mind and receive it as statements, sounds, a song or lyric, or sensed as a vibration. It is the easiest of all the intuitive abilities because you can hear it. Clairaudients receive their intuitive information through an area located just above their ears but below the temples. This area of the brain covers the temporal lobes, which is where we process auditory information.

Everybody can identify with that "little voice" in the back of their minds. We all know what our own voice sounds like inside our head.

We all "talk" to ourselves. We've all had at least one instance in our life where we've heard that little voice inside our minds warning us of danger. We also "hear" our egos nattering away at us all the time. The difficult part for clairaudients is learning how to discern the difference between intuitive guidance and the ego voice. As a result, people who are predominantly clairaudient will be the first to question everything they "hear," because for them, it's like they are only thinking out loud. Pete Sanders, Jr., notes in his book, *You are Psychic,* that because this voice sounds so familiar, those of us who are predominantly clairaudient struggle with the validity of what is being said. He refers to it as "a credibility gap" as a result of this inner confusion between the ego voice and the voice of the inner calm (87).

Clairaudients are so comfortable with the sound of their own voice that they only learn the difference between their ego voice and their intuitive voice when they can identify the difference in tone with the information they are hearing.

The intuitive voice, which is the inner calm, is calm, loving, subtle, and in times of danger, very strong and direct. It empowers you and gives you confidence. The ego voice, on the other hand, is critical, demanding, demeaning, and authoritative; it can be quite harsh and has the tendency to make you feel powerless. When we are in the throes of the "monkey mind," it can be hard to hear the calm intuitive voice of love and reason. For this reason, clairaudients garner the greatest benefits from meditating on a regular basis, as it helps them to discern between the ego voice and the voice of their intuition.

Clairaudients can read other people's energy by what they "hear." Years ago when I was on a training course learning a new healing technique, I met a woman who was a very talented musician. She could "hear" auras and could tell you what color your aura was based on the tone of musical note she heard. If the music had a flat tone or sharp tone, she knew the body was out of balance. If she heard a harmonic tone, she would know that area of the body was in balance.

If you ask someone who is clairaudient if they would like an orange, they will hear a yes or no inside their minds.

Claircognizance

Claircognizance is called "clear knowing." Claircognizants see or perceive intuitive information as a hunch or through an impression where they know what the answer is. Of all the intuitive abilities, this one is the strongest because the claircognizant receives information instantly and will know what will or will not work.

Claircognizants receive their information through one of two areas in the body, either the heart chakra or the crown chakra. The heart chakra is located in the middle of your chest just above the tip of your breastbone. The crown chakra is located at the top of your head.

This intuitive information can be perceived as a warm feeling that emanates from the chest, or it can be felt like a rush through the top of the head and received as complete ideas or statements. Men, for example, have a strong tendency to be claircognizants because they trust their "hunches or instincts." A person who is considered a good judge of character is often very claircognizant. Someone who has prophetic dreams or visions of future events can be very claircognizant.

When I was about eight years old, I remember stepping out onto our front porch and looking up at the trees. At that moment I had a vision. I "saw" myself walking down the aisle of a church. I could see that I was wearing a wedding dress and caught a glimpse of the man I was going to marry. I felt happy and content. I knew I was to "wait for him." When I met my husband, I knew that this was the man I was going to marry by the end of our first date, but I didn't relate it back to the vision I had as a child. A few months later we attended a friend's wedding at his church. As the bride walked down the aisle, I remember looking up at the ceiling of the church and that's when it hit me that "this is the church I will marry in." My whole body tingled and vibrated. We had only been dating for a few months when we decided to marry. There was some opposition to our marrying so quickly, and to be honest, we were both a little nervous. When I "remembered" my vision at that moment in the church, any questions or concerns I had about marrying him instantly faded away.

If you ask a claircognizant if they would like an orange to eat, they will have a sense of what it would be like to have one or not.

What Type of Intuitive Are You?

By now you are probably getting a sense of where you fit in the intuitive spectrum of things. I am sure you would like a little more confirmation, though. Here is a short quiz to help you determine what type of an intuitive you are.

Before you take the quiz, remember you have all four abilities, but one or two of them will be predominant. Once you find out what your dominant skill is, you will be able to focus on that ability and develop it until it becomes second nature.

You will need a pen and paper to do the quiz. Take a deep breath, relax, and release any need or expectations. Have some fun with this.

🪷 Exercise 🪷
Discovering Your Dominant Intuitive Skill Quiz

Read the following statements below and choose either a, b, c, or d. You can have more than one choice, so put down all the letters that resonate with you.

1. When you return from a vacation, are you more apt to describe:
    a. What you saw? (Scenery, architecture, people, culture)
    b. How you felt? (Relaxed, happy, miserable, smell of the flowers)
    c. What you heard? (Music, conversations, wildlife, sounds of the ocean)
    d. What you learned about the area? (Customs, history, museums, language)
2. When you finish watching a movie, are your first thoughts about:
    a. The cinematography, clothes, scenery? (Feel like you are immersed in the story)
    b. The emotions you felt? (Laughed until I cried, sad, tense, frustrated)
    c. The sound track? (Loved the music, aware of every sound or track played, bought the soundtrack)
    d. The message in the movie? (Symbolism, concepts, accuracy of the story)

3. When you plan your next vacation, will you pick locations based on:

>   a. Visuals? (Lush beaches, romantic villas, places to explore)

>   b. How you feel in the moment? (I need a vacation, stressed, anxious, have to get out of here, need to escape for a while)

>   c. Activities (Musical events, concerts, guided tours)

>   d. History (What can I learn? What can I do to help?)

4. When you listen to the radio, do you:

>   a. Visualize the singer and the band or remember images from the video?

>   b. Really get into the music and feel it?

>   c. Play along in your head and know every note or bar of music that is being played?

>   d. Listen to the message? Is there a story or a meaning, or is it repetitive?

5. When you read a book, are you:

>   a. Inside the story? You can feel yourself and the characters having the conversation

>   b. Feel the emotions of the characters and begin to identify with one or the group?

>   c. Hear the sounds implied by the story? (Band music played in the background, the sound of the carriage on the cobble stone road, the roar of the lion or the sound of the sea crashing onto the beach)

>   d. Looking for symbolism in the book? What is the author really trying to say? What is the moral of the story?

How to Interpret Your Answers:

If you answered:

>   A: For all five questions then you are predominately a clairvoyant (clear seeing)

>   B: For all five questions then you are predominately a clairsentient (clear feeling)

C: For all five questions then you are predominately a clairaudient (clear hearing)

D: For all five questions then you are predominately a claircognizant (clear sensing)

If you discover that your answers have varied, look at the combinations. If you have three of one and two of another, then you are predominately the answer you gave three times, with the other answer being present but not as dominate. I would recommend you pick one that resonates the most closely for you and focus on that one first. When you are comfortable with that intuitive ability, go back and focus on your other intuitive ability. It will be good training for you to understand the difference between them and how they work for you.

After a short period of time, you will begin to realize that you do in fact have all four. This will come with practice as you learn how to "read" information intuitively.

To give you some context, when I did the quiz, my answer was A for three questions and D for two of the questions. This means that I am predominately a clairvoyant with strong claircognizant abilities. For me, A is more natural, so I focused on mastering that ability first. Then I focused on claircognizance. Now I use both at the same time. I can see an image in my mind's eye and then I get an interpretation or hunch happening in my heart, or sometimes I feel it coming down through the top of my head. The majority of the time they happen together.

Now that you have an understanding of what type of an intuitive you are, things should become clearer for you. Treat it like an adventure and see how you can apply your intuition to the different aspects your life. Each intuitive ability has its advantages and disadvantages. When you are aware of your intuitive abilities you are more closely aligned with your inner calm. When you are out of step with your intuitive abilities, then your ego is having some fun calling the shots. Being able to feel the difference is all part of the dance. To help you master your intuitive talent a bit further, I have also included some interesting exercises below. They are fun and easy to do. As you do the exercises, you may find that writing down what you are sensing and feeling in a journal will be quite useful. It will also help you track how your skill set as an intuitive is developing over time. Going back over your results might surprise you.

The Clairvoyant Dance

Clairvoyants are visual people. They love to take a gazillion pictures and always need to buy extra memory cards for their cameras. They are creative, love colors, and they always seem to be involved in some sort of craft, such as scrapbooking, painting, or quilting, etc. Their homes are filled with art and decorated in beautiful colors. Their surroundings are orderly because messes drive them crazy. They are the shoppers who always pick up the perfect vase or just the right piece of jewelry to go with the dress they bought last year. In business, clairvoyants have a knack for being able to visualize how a project will turn out before it even starts. Seeing the big picture is easy for them, and they can foresee what will work or what will hold a project up. CEOs of large corporations often have this gift of visualization.

One company I worked with asked me to reorganize their department and come up with a better layout for the staff. Turns out there were a group of engineers working together who knew if a piece of furniture could fit in a room just by looking at it. They could visualize space, dimension, volume, depth, and placement, and all I had to do was show them a picture of a chair or desk. It was amazing to watch. They were never wrong. It saved me a lot of time when I was reorganizing their department to make room for a new addition.

Being a clairvoyant can also be a bit of a problem because you can sometimes just blurt things out without meaning to. I ran into this little problem all the time. As you get used to your ability, you'll be able to filter yourself more clearly. Once, while having lunch with some of my coworkers, I had a flash in my mind's eye of one of the ladies holding a sick baby that seemed to be running a high fever. I turned and looked at her and asked, "How is your baby doing?" She was surprised by the question and said the baby is great.

With surprise in my voice I said, "Oh."

Curious, she asked me why I wanted to know, and I replied, "Oh, I just wanted to make sure that the baby was okay." She looked puzzled and I felt embarrassed. That question just popped out of my mouth and I didn't think it through. You could tell it upset her.

The next day when I came into work I found out that she'd spent the entire night in the hospital with the baby. The baby had suddenly spiked a high fever and had a seizure that night. Thankfully the baby was okay.

🪷 Exercise 🪷

Practice Using Your Clairvoyance with These Simple Exercises

To locate the clairvoyant receptor inside the middle of your forehead, close your eyes and focus on the area between your eyes. Imagine or pretend that you are inside the middle of your brain and looking out through an imaginary eye. This area is also called the third eye.

1. Think about a memory that made you happy. Write out the memory and observe how you "see" it in your mind's eye. Is it in color or black and white? Does the story replay scene by scene or is it like a movie playing in your mind? Write out how you are seeing it.

2. When you read a book, are you inside the story? Do you live it? Does it create images in your mind of what the characters look like or talk like? Is it a movie or images that flash through your mind? Is it in color or black and white?

3. Think about a movie you saw that you really loved. How do you remember it? Can you see scenes from the movie flash before your eyes? Is thinking about the movie like being back in the theater and watching it all over again, or do you feel yourself sitting on the couch in the front of the TV watching the movie? Is it in color or black and white?

What's the Inner Calm to Being Clairvoyant?

Clairvoyants are the big picture thinkers (seeing from the fifty-thousand foot view) who can easily see finished outcomes on a project before they are completed. They are excellent organizers (have a tendency to rearrange furniture a lot), excellent problem solvers because they can see more than one solution to a problem, love time management (systems, graphs, charts), love to make lists, have a great sense of direction, and they rarely get lost.

What Is the Ego of Being Clairvoyant?

Clairvoyants can be resistant to change, inflexible, and arrogant. They always believe they are right and have to have the last word. They are perfectionists (cannot tolerate mistakes or clutter), worriers, judgmental, critical, and they tend to meddle in other people's problems. Clairvoyants will jump to conclusions before they have all the facts.

Meditating while focusing on this area between your eyes can be a very powerful way to further expand your clairvoyant abilities. You may eventually experience a mystic event where all of a sudden you find an eye opening up and looking back at you. As you look at your inner eye, you will feel peaceful and loving as it looks back at you. It doesn't happen for everyone, so don't be concerned if it doesn't happen to you. However, if it does, I want to make sure you understand why. Know that it is a natural event for intuitives.

Theosophy, ancient philosophers, and other Eastern religions have taught that the third eye is connected to the pineal gland, which is considered to be the seat of the soul. Ancient tribes found ways to stimulate this gland to assist in realizing higher realms of understanding and consciousness. For over a thousand years, the pineal gland has traditionally been represented as a pinecone. Physical evidence of this symbol can be found in ancient hieroglyphs, paintings, and statues from many different cultures from around the world, including esoteric Christianity.

Scientists were surprised to find that when the pineal gland was examined under a microscope, it was in fact shaped like a pinecone and contained the same elements of rods and cones like a human eye has. This provides us with further evidence that the pineal gland is an organ of vision.[1]

When I was touring the Vatican a few years ago, I was quite fascinated to find a huge statue of a pinecone fountain located in the Court of the Pinecone. The fountain was originally built by the Romans in the first century and was situated near the Pantheon next to the Temple of Isis. It was moved to Vatican City in the Middle Ages and was flanked by two peacocks, one on each side, which are the esoteric symbols for immortality. I found it to be an interesting social statement—an Eastern religion's mystical reference to the seat of the soul that is surrounded by symbols of immortality in the courtyard of one of the most powerful Christian churches in the world.

The Clairsentient Dance

Being predominately clairsentient means that you can feel or sense things. Feelings can be powerful motivators and can create strong physical reactions anywhere in the body, such as gut aches or body clues. Clairsentients are very compassionate and empathic people. They always just know the right thing to say or do. It is a gift. They ooze love, gentleness, and tenderness. Little children just love to sit on their laps and get hugs. I always thought that Glinda, the good witch of the North in *The Wizard of Oz*, personified a clairsentient.

Clairsentients can also receive intuitive insights in the form of tastes or smells. One client of mine who owned a retail store told me that she could always tell when she was working with a customer who was angry about something. She told me, "I always smell smoke when someone is angry."

In my practice I see two primary types of clairsentients. The first type of clairsentient receives their intuitive insights through what are called "body clues." Once clairsentients recognize what a body cue is, their life will become much easier and they will be less anxious.

---

1. There is ongoing debate that the third eye is in fact connected to the pituitary gland, which is also referred to as the master gland. I am open minded about the possibility but still defer to my Theosophical teachings that have always referred to the pineal gland as being connected to the third eye.

Clairsentients who get body clues have a tendency to be what I lovingly refer to as little human Velcros. They pick up everybody's energy and then don't know what else to do with it. They carry it around in their field and then start to think that they:

A) caused it

B) created it

C) have to fix it—A confusing dilemma to say the least!

Years ago I was having lunch with a friend and I suddenly got this toothache. It had come on so fast that it threw me off. My friend looked at me and asked me if I was all right. I said, "I think I need to call the dentist. I have a toothache." My friend looked surprised and said, "Wow, I just came from the dentist. I had a root canal this morning. My tooth is still sore." That caused me to pause. So I asked myself silently if what I was feeling was really her toothache. That's when I realized I was feeling her pain too. Once I silently acknowledged that to myself, my toothache mysteriously disappeared. That saved me some money. If I had not acknowledged my toothache in that way, I could have very well been on a merry goose chase for a tooth that wasn't sore.

The second type of clairsentient receives their intuitive insights through the solar plexus, or belly, and it is called having a "gut ache." It is often confused with nervousness or a digestive problem. It can be accompanied with diarrhea and nausea in extreme cases. People report it as feeling like they were punched in the stomach or suddenly felt weak and had to sit down. Young children have a tendency to be very clairsentient, especially if they are sensitive and emotional. These are the children that often come home from school complaining of bellyaches. Trips to the doctor often reveal that they are fine and parents are told the child is making it all up. The reality is that their child is feeling someone else's emotions and don't know what to do about it. At no point does anyone ask the child if they are feeling unhappy or concerned about something going on at school or if there has been some conflict with a little friend. Doing so would eliminate a great deal of unhappiness for everyone involved.

Feeling hungry or full is just one very simple example of clairsentience, believe it or not. Unfortunately, our determination to validate anything with scientific proof has interfered with our intuitive senses, and so we learn to ignore them. For example, most of us have been taught to clean up our plates because there are starving children in Africa. As a result, we clean our plates regardless of whether our body wants to eat that much or if we aren't feeling well that day. How many times have you, as a child, been forced to finish your dinner only to get sick later because you were coming down with the flu? I often find that my clients who have developed an eating disorder are very clairsentient. My clients, in turn, are often surprised to find that the root of their eating disorder is an early childhood memory where they have been forced to eat something that made them feel ill. People who are bulimics tend to swallow their emotions or the emotions of others and are only able to release the pain and emotion that doesn't belong to them by vomiting it out.

I find in my practice that people who are afraid of crowds or have panic attacks in public places are also highly sensitive clairsentients. They become overwhelmed by other people's energy and feelings and then short circuit. Their egos have them convinced that what they are feeling is theirs. Once they learn how to discern what they are feeling from what other people are feeling, they do just fine.

🪷 Exercise 🪷
Practice Your Clairsentience with These Simple Exercises

The clairsentient receptor area is located in the middle of the belly in the area between the diaphragm and the bellybutton, also called the solar plexus chakra or the third chakra. Clairsentients are also very gifted at feeling things anywhere in their body. They can receive information as body clues or gut aches. Remember—these sensations can feel so real that they can often be mistaken for being your own and treated like a symptom.

1. Do you remember getting gut aches when you were a child in school? Do you feel sick if you have to do something that scares you? Do you suffer from diarrhea or nausea before a big presentation? Describe the feeling of the gut ache? Where exactly do you feel it in your body? Above or below the belly button? Does the feeling have a color or taste to it? (Gut ache)

2. Write out an example of where you were feeling somebody else's pain and were surprised to find out it was coming from them. Example: when you arrived at work you were feeling fine, but you felt a headache coming on while you had lunch with your coworker. You mentioned the headache to your friend only to find that she had a headache too. (Body clue)

3. Think of an instance in your life when you have really felt something was off and you couldn't figure out what it was. An example would be attending a party and talking to someone who makes you feel tired or sick. What was the experience like? What happened as a result? Where did you feel it?

What's the Inner Calm to Being Clairsentient?

People who are predominately clairsentient are the most loving, empathic, and compassionate people, and they make the finest of best friends. They have a knack of always being in the right place at the right time, and they know just what to say or do. They love good food, good wine, and are usually amazing cooks. They trust their feelings, they are the best cuddlers (kiddie and pet magnets), they are party pleasers, and they live in comfortable homes that always seem to look a little disorganized.

What's the Ego to Being Clairsentient?

Clairsentients ruled by their egos will pick up everybody's stuff. (Remember—they are emotional Velcros.) They are worriers, they are easily overwhelmed, they can have a fear of crowds, and they can often experience anxiety. They will cry easily and will feel rejected if you forget to smile at them (needing a lot of reassurance all the time).

They can't make deadlines and they live in constant chaos, forever losing their keys and phones. They often have digestive issues and want to hide in their homes. They look disheveled and disorganized. Their desks, cars, and homes are messy, which can eventually develop into hoarding.

The Clairaudient Dance

Clairaudients receive their intuitive guidance through words and phrases heard inside their minds. There is no questioning that magical little voice in the back of your mind. We all talk to ourselves. We know what "we" sound like inside our own heads. People who are predominately clairaudient find listening to their intuition the easiest. In my workshops, all participants report having at least one instance in their life where they "heard" a voice from within warning them of danger.

Clairaudients are very sensitive to sound. They love good music, the sound of the wind, the waves, birds singing, people laughing. They have the best music collection and audio equipment. They have a very low tolerance of squeaky hinges, static, and sounds that are jarring and irritating. They tend to crave silence after a busy day, especially if they have been exposed to a lot of ambient noise throughout the day.

Intuitive hearing also evokes the strongest emotional memories for people. We might not recall who attended our first school dance or what clothing we wore, but there is a chance we will remember the song that played when we had that first dance. Christmas of 1964 will always bring special memories for me because our mother bought us our own record player. She bought us the hit single "Downtown" by Petula Clark. Even today, hearing that song takes me back to memories of sitting on the floor with my sister while we played with our dolls.

🪷 Exercise 🪷
Practice Your Clairaudience with These Simple Exercises

The clairaudient receptor area is located just above the ears but below the temples. If you place your middle finger at the outside edge of your eyes and place your thumb over your ear canal, your index finger will mark the area in the middle. This area can also be a little tender to the touch. A clairaudient should focus on hearing through this area as opposed to hearing through their ears.

1. Write out some of your musical memories. Do you remember the song that was playing the first time you danced with someone? What was "your" song on your wedding day? What song always brings back a beautiful memory for you?

2. Write out a memory of an instance where you heard a word or a warning that came true. For example: being out with friends and suddenly hearing a shout of danger that came out of nowhere that saved you. Was there a time when you think you heard someone tell you to call home because something was wrong, and it turned out to be true?

3. There are two types of hearing. One is called outer hearing and the other is called inner hearing. To practice outer hearing, sit in silence and record all the things you hear going on around you outside. An example would be birds singing, traffic, or people passing on the street. To practice inner hearing, sit in silence, listen to your thoughts, and write them down. Now shift from outer hearing to inner hearing and back again. Write down how it feels. Shifting back and forth can sometimes feel like a shift in pressure.

What's the Inner Calm to Being Clairaudient?

Being clairaudient is the best intuitive ability for understanding and receiving intuitive guidance or receiving specific answers to questions. They are articulate, they think before they speak, they are usually musically inclined, and they can be multilingual, and they always have the best playlists for parties. They rarely feel overwhelmed and can tune people in or out. Clairaudients are often the quiet one standing in the corner listening to everything.

What's the Ego to being Clairaudient?

When they are being ruled by their egos, clairaudients have a hard time trusting their inner guidance because they don't trust "the voices" inside their head. They have difficulty understanding the difference between fear and intuition and cannot tolerate ambient noises. They are the least likely to trust themselves, but they can also come on too strong. Clairaudients love the sound of their own voice and need people to listen to them. They can become screamers, having constant problems with their hearing. They have a tendency to take conversations out of context. They like seclusion and want to be left alone a lot, because silence is the only thing that feels safe.

The Claircognizant Dance

Being claircognizant means having the ability to know things. The "knowing" can be so fleeting you can react instantaneously without even realizing it. There is nothing to support what you know with anything tangible, it just is. This is called having a hunch. A statement that claircognizants often make is "I know that" or "I knew that was going to happen." It is considered to be the driving force behind the fight or flight response when there is danger.

Claircognizants are quick thinkers, fast movers, and are often considered quite prophetic. They know what people are going to say and do and how things will turn out long before anyone else does. They have a knack for being the right person in the right place at the right time. They can tell you what time of day it is without looking at their watch. They are always well prepared and ahead of the trend, or they are the trendsetters. They are quick-witted, engaging, and entertaining. They can be the life of the party.

My father had good hunches. He was considered by everyone in the family to be a very astute judge of character. I learned to not object too much when he ran boyfriends off. Eventually I would find out that the guy he wouldn't let me date was not all that great. Between my intuition and my father's gut instincts, guys didn't stand much of a chance. My husband was the only man my father ever approved of. I had a hunch my father would approve of him, and he did. We are still happily married thirty-seven years later.

With that same sense of knowing, I knew I was going to have a boy, but I didn't know it wasn't going to be my first pregnancy. I knew the day that my daughter was going to be born. That little piece of information was useful because my husband Bert had to unexpectedly go out of town on business on my due date. It didn't stop me from crying all the way to the airport, mind you, but I knew deep down he would be back in time. He was.

🌸 Exercise 🌸
Practice Your Claircognizance with These Simple Exercises
The claircognizant receptor area is located in the chest area or heart chakra (fourth chakra) but it can also be felt at the top of the head or crown chakra (seventh chakra).

1. Write out an example when you just knew something was going to happen and it did. This is also called having déjà vu. It can be an event, a conversation, or a situation you found yourself in.
2. Think of a time when you just knew you were doing something wrong but did it anyway. How did it feel? Where did you feel it in your body? How did you feel afterward? Have you found that since that experience you are more open to your hunches?
3. Have you ever been somewhere and suddenly felt you needed to get out of there? Describe the event and how it felt. Where did you feel it in your body? How did you feel afterward? What happened as a result of that experience?

What's the Inner Calm to Being Claircognizant
People who are predominately claircognizant are quick thinkers, spontaneous, adaptable, and strong negotiators who have a reputation for their astute instincts. They react quickly to danger, can usually sense the future outcome of an event, have lots of synchronicity in their lives, and are the best host or hostesses. They always seem to know when things will work out and will leave things to the last minute. They are leaders and are self-assured and confident. They have great instincts and are easily trusted by others.

What's the Ego to Being Claircognizant?

A claircognizant being dominated by his or her ego has a hard time trusting their instincts. They have difficulty fitting into groups because they can come across as being rude, impatient, or arrogant know-it-alls who have a low tolerance for fools. They rarely finish what they start, never read the instruction manual, and won't ask for directions.

🪷 Exercise 🪷
Practicing Your Intuition with Games

Other fun things you can do to further develop your intuition is to play games. For example, every time the phone rings, see if you can intuitively determine who is calling. Helpful tip: a clairvoyant may see the face of the person flash in their minds eye, a clairsentient will feel the presence or essence of the person, a clairaudient will hear their name, and a claircognizant will just know who it is.

Another game you can play to hone your intuitive skill set is playing with a deck of cards. Take a full deck of cards and sit quietly for a moment while you shuffle the deck. Let yourself feel the energy surrounding the deck. Now take a moment to decide what a red card feels like using your strongest intuitive ability. Then decide what a black card will feel like. Now, keeping each card face down, pull the first card from the top of the deck and before you turn it over, intuitively decide what color it is. Then turn it over and see if you are right. Go with your first impression. Don't second-guess yourself. Repeat this nine times. Remember your ego will try to get you to change your answers. Helpful tip: A clairvoyant will see red or black flash in their minds eye, a clairsentient will feel if the card is red or black, a clairaudient will hear the word red or black, and claircognizant will know if the card is red or black.

Even if you only get one card right, you are well on your way. Remember it takes time for you to learn how to understand how to read the cards based on your dominant intuitive gift. Have some fun playing with the cards. Try playing them with your children and see what happens. It could be quite fascinating.

Dancing with Your Intuition

Now you know why you know things.

Remember that this is a natural gift and half the battle will be giving yourself the permission to relax and learn how to use it. Use the games to practice and enhance your intuitive gifts. The more you practice, the easier it will become. A helpful hint: intuitive flashes are very quick and instantaneous. You have to learn how to catch them and trust them. The more you practice and play with your intuition, the easier it will get.

Find ways to incorporate your newfound innate gift into your day-to-day life. Start with the simple things and work your way up. I found writing things down in a journal at the end of the day really helped me to be aware of when I used my intuition and when I didn't use it. The more I became aware of how much I was using it, the more confident I became. It really is a simple matter of developing your confidence. You may also find it very helpful to not tell anyone you are practicing. People might be afraid to validate your hunches or instincts. Over time you will see if you are right or not. It is more productive to just stand back to see what the outcome is. As they say, "the proof is in the pudding." You don't need to prove to anyone you are intuitive. You only need to give yourself permission to be intuitive.

As you read through this book, you will find that there are many techniques and exercises here to help you to understand how to use your intuitive talent more effectively. As your confidence in your intuitive abilities gets stronger you will find that you are much more in touch with the inner calm. It will be harder for your ego to banter and push you around because that calm inner voice will just nod and do what feels right anyway. I started to recognize over time that my ego voice was just a scared little kid who didn't know any better. I started to see my intuition, that inner calm voice, as the adult who could stand back and calmly assess the situation. My inner calm could listen to the rant of the scared little kid and then help it see the situation in a different light.

Over time you will discover what a gift your intuition is. "Learning is finding out what you already know. Doing is demonstrating that you know it. Teaching is reminding others that they know just as well as you. You are all learners, doers, and teachers" (Bach). Listening to your intuition will get you there. Learning when and how to use it will help you become accustomed to making it a natural part of who you are.

3

The Ethics of Intuition

Learning how to dance with your intuition is very important. Otherwise, it can become a burden and create a lot of unnecessary stress and anxiety in your life. You could begin to see it as a curse, which would be a shame because it is a gift. Learning how to use your intuition appropriately will make your life much richer, calmer, and more peaceful and fulfilling. I have developed some guidelines to help you understand how and when to use it. I call the set of guidelines "Intuitive Ethics."

As I started to dance with my intuition, I realized that the internal mental chatter of my ego was always going to be there, but I didn't have to listen to it. It was more important to pay attention to how my intuition was guiding me. This shifted my focus away from the constant prattle of the ego voice. As I practiced this, I noticed that my ego voice started to slide into the background, like static on a radio. I could tune into the frenetic ego voice or tune into my intuition and its calm wisdom. Doing this helped me understand the dance between my ego fears and the inner calm of my intuitive mind. The more I allowed myself to dance between the two, the easier life became. It started to become second nature.

My dance instructor refers to this kind of remembering as "muscle memory." It becomes so much a part of you that you don't even have to think about it anymore, it is just a natural reflex. Acknowledging the difference between my ego and my inner calm took me years to figure out, but once I did—wow—what a difference it made in my personal life and my career. Life got a whole lot easier.

Six Concepts for Practicing Intuition Ethically

As I started to trust what I was feeling and sensing, I learned that how I handled my intuition was very important. Listening to my intuition reduced my stress when I used it properly. My anxiety would increase when I used it inappropriately. Understanding the difference of when and how to use it was the next piece of the intuitive dance.

In the beginning, I made the mistake of thinking that I had to get proof of what I was picking up from the other person. When I asked for validation, I quickly learned that it just freaked them out, and they would avoid me. If, on the other hand, I just followed what I was feeling and acted on it in a quiet way, the other person always appreciated my compassion and understanding.

For example, if they were acting happy but were really sad underneath, I didn't need to inquire about the sadness, I just needed to support the happiness. I could leave the sadness alone and not feel responsible for it or think I had created it. It taught me that I didn't have to say anything; I just needed to change how I was reacting to a situation based on what my intuition was telling me. I was learning about free will and the power of choice. This awareness helped me to develop proper manners with regards to my intuition. It was also helping me to be clear about my emotional boundaries.

The "Intuitive Ethics" are:

1. Just because you think you know, doesn't mean you do.
2. Wait to be asked.
3. Only do as you're asked.
4. If you are not asked, but wish to help, send love silently and hand it over to God.
5. Ask, "Is this mine?" or "Does it belong to someone else?"
6. Be honest.

I have relied on these six concepts for years. After I formally developed them, I wrote them out onto cue cards. I had those suckers taped up all over the place. They were taped up by every phone in the house, placed on the wall of my home office, and taped to the side of my computer. I wanted to be sure I remembered these concepts until they were muscle memory. Over time, the more I practiced them the more I noticed the changes it made to my personal relationships. In some cases the changes were really quite dramatic.

For example, when I started to incorporate these intuitive ethics into my conversations with my children who were away at university, it became a serious game changer in my relationship with them. Not only did it reduce my stress and anxiety big time, but the kids were much less argumentative when they came home on weekends. They started to call home more often as well.

As time went on I found that I was beginning to automatically use these same intuitive principles in my office with clients. They were so successful that I started to apply them when I was talking to friends or family members. When my mother died, my sister and I had to deal with some pretty extreme drama from outside the family circle. Applying these intuitive ethics allowed me to be crystal clear about my boundaries, giving me clarity on requests that we received. It saved both my sister and I a lot of unnecessary grief. I realized later how much it also saved my sanity and gave me the space to grieve.

God's greatest gift to us is free will and choice. As I started to respect my free will and the choices I was making for myself, I recognized that other people were doing exactly the same thing. Actively honoring free will and choice helped me develop healthy emotional boundaries for myself and respect them in others. I became more tolerant, less judgmental, more observant, and willing to listen. It created the space I needed to love myself and to love others from a place without judgment.

1. Just Because You Think You Know Doesn't Mean You Do

This means that just because you think you know intuitively how to solve someone's problem doesn't mean you have their permission to share any advice with them. Your opinion has not been requested. Honor their choices and free will.

If a friend, loved one, or colleague is struggling with a problem and they have chosen to share it with you, your intuition is naturally going to offer up numerous solutions. It is extremely difficult to not want to help them or try to fix it or save them. Intuitively sensing or feeling what might solve the problem does not give you permission to share your feelings on the subject.

They didn't ask for help. They need someone compassionate to talk too. Don't judge. You never know the whole story. My mother always used to say "Mind your own beeswax." This tactic, by the way, does not apply to life threatening situations. We are only dealing with emotional issues here.

Remember: Just because you think you know doesn't mean you do! Honor their free will.

Well that sounds just plain heartless, you may say.

Does it?

Think back on how many times you have had a personal issue you have been dealing with and you called up a friend because you needed to talk it out. How often did your dear friend just start telling you what they thought you should do about it? How did it make you feel?

We all do it from time to time. We love to help people but we don't stop and ask if they want help. We just assume they are asking for help because they are telling us. Let's take a look at an example of how this can play out.

Your girlfriend Sally calls and wants to meet you for lunch. She sounds upset and naturally you feel concerned. You know that she has been having a tough time at work and she and her boss don't see eye to eye on a big project they are working on together. When you meet her, she looks happy enough, but you can intuitively feel her agitation and begin to pick up that there is something very wrong. Soon enough your friend starts to talk about some of the problems she is having with her boss at work. Intuitively you know exactly what she is going through and have solutions to offer. Naturally, as her friend, you feel the need to help her with her problem. You just can't wait to share all your advice, so you begin to make a stream of suggestions. You ask Sally if she has tried this or that. You keep talking and encouraging her to try different things that you believe will help solve her problem. But Sally isn't responding the way you think she should. Sally starts to make excuses on why she can't do anything you have suggested. You get agitated because you just know that "if she followed my advice, then all her problems would be resolved." Your friend, on the other hand, doesn't know what to do with all the advice. She isn't sure she is ready to follow your advice and she doesn't want to offend you by not doing so. Sally changes the subject and you both feel uncomfortable. She doesn't want to offend you because she loves you, and you can't understand why she isn't as thrilled as you are with all your marvelous suggestions. You love her and want the best for her.

The problem here is that she didn't ask you for advice!

Just because you think you know, doesn't mean you do.

What's the best way to handle that? I learned to listen and then ask, "Are you asking for any advice or do you just need me to listen?"

2. Wait to Be Asked

"Wait to be asked" means just that—waiting to be asked for help. This sets a very clear emotional boundary. You are making it clear that you are present and listening. You are respecting their space and letting them decide how and when they want help.

It doesn't mean, however, that you can't ask if you *may* offer to make some suggestions. If they accept your offer and say yes, then I recommend offering several different solutions and letting them choose what would work best for them. This empowers them to find the right solution for them. It honors their own free will. Remember, you never know the full story.

If, on the other hand, they decline your offer and say no, accept their decision with grace and don't push for a reason. Don't take it personally. Not everyone can hear solutions when they are upset and overwhelmed.

Listening to a dear friend's emotional struggles can be agonizing because the helper in you wants so badly to help resolve the problem.

You can see how much Sally is suffering and you empathize with her. You can feel her pain and you can know intuitively what the perfect solution is.

Let's go back to Sally's problem and see how this could be handled using the "Intuitive Ethics" and waiting to be asked.

Your friend arrives for lunch and you can feel her agitation. You can feel her pain, and with love you express your concern to Sally. She begins to tell you what is happening at work and how she just doesn't know what to do about it. Your intuition kicks in and starts to map out solutions for Sally. You want to share. You want to help.

Instead of jumping in and giving her solutions, ask Sally, "Are you asking me for help, or do you just need someone to listen?"

This sets a very clear boundary for her and for you. It lets her know that you are willing to help but willing to respect her choices. You are honoring her free will and respecting her choices on the matter.

If your friend responds, "No, I just need someone to talk to," accept it with grace and just let them talk. You are already offering support just by being there to listen. For some people that is all they need at the time. This is honoring.

By respecting your friend's wishes and just listening, as hard as that may be, your job at this point is to stay present and listen. By doing so you are giving yourself permission to be the empathic friend who can listen without judgment. She in turn can talk freely knowing that she is not being judged or counseled when she isn't ready to hear what you have to say. If she wants your advice, wait for her to ask.

If, on the other hand, your friend responds with, "Yes, I would be interested in what you think I should do." Offer her several solutions. I like to say, "Well, I see you might have several different options. You could do a, b, or c." Then I will say, "What feels right for you?" or "What do you think will work for you?"

This hands the problem back to the friend and it demonstrates that you trust her. You are empowering her to find her own solutions. You are honoring her free will and you are being empathic and compassionate by loving her enough to not interfere with her path in life.

3. Only Do as Asked

"Only do as asked" means that if you are asked to help, make sure you understand what you are being asked to help with. If someone asks me for help, I make them spell it out. I can't tell you how many times I have been asked to help with something and I just assume they would want it done a certain way, only later to find out that I had it all wrong. Just because I am intuitive doesn't mean I get it right all the time. I am always the person who shows up with too much food, for example. Being asked to bring some food to a party doesn't mean they are asking you to feed the entire party! I have learned to ask, regardless of what I feel is the right thing to do.

But what do you do if they don't want help? What do you do if they just want you to listen and not offer any suggestions of any kind?

4. If You Are Not Asked, Send Love

"If you are not asked, send love" means that if you are not asked for advice or help, then remain present, knowing that you are honoring their decision and their free will. This is the hardest one of all. The friend just wants you to listen. They don't want any help, haven't asked for it, and can't accept it, so you cannot offer. This is honoring their right to choose what is best for them. It is not your decision, regardless of how you feel about the current state of affairs.

In this situation, all you can do is sit back, listen, and just keep repeating "I love you" silently to yourself inside your mind. You will find that they start to calm down, as will you. The divine order of life will take care of the rest.

It is truly agonizing to sit back and watch someone you love struggle. If it is a loved one who continues to stay in an abusive situation, there is little you can do except be there for them. It is hard to walk by a homeless person and send them love when it makes you feel angry that they are in that position. It is agonizing for any parent to stand back and watch a child make the same mistake over and over again.

When I was about eight years old, my sister decided that she wanted to make herself a stool to sit on. I don't remember why. She felt it was important and wanted to do it all by herself. My mother said fine and showed her where to find the wood, nails, and a hammer, and then she walked away to leave her to it. I can remember sitting upstairs in our apartment and listening to my sister yelling and screaming at those pieces of wood downstairs in my father's shop. She could not figure out how to make the stool stand up by itself. She was at it for hours. She howled and raged and banged away at the wood. I finally said to my mother, "Shouldn't we help her?" My mother said, "No, let her figure it out for herself. She hasn't asked for help." Well, she did eventually figure it out, and boy was she proud.

All you can do is wait for them to ask and be there for them when they do ask. We have no idea what lesson their soul is trying to learn by repeating the same pattern over and over again. It is not for us to judge, only to stay present in love.

There are exceptions to this rule. If someone is about to harm themselves or someone else, that is a totally different matter.

5. Is This Mine? Or Does It Belong to Someone Else?

This means checking in with your intuition to make sure that what you are feeling is actually yours. This intuitive ethic is particularly critical for those of you who are predominately clairsentient (emotional Velcro). As I have said earlier, most of what intuitives react to emotionally and personally has nothing to do with them. I have seen evidence of this in my practice for years, which is why I developed this concept.

If you are upset or feel unwell, always ask yourself first, "Is this mine? Or does it belong to someone else?" Remember body cues. If you get into the habit of questioning your physical and emotional responses to things, I think you will be quite surprised to find that most of it isn't yours to begin with.

Remember: No matter what you are feeling physically, emotionally, or mentally, ask yourself, "Is this mine? Or does it belong to someone else?" You are looking for the Velcro and body cues here.

If your response to the question is unsure, then it is not yours. You don't need to know where it came from or why, let it go. Don't let your ego make you think you either caused it, created it, or have to fix it.

You only need to be aware that your intuition is aware of it and it doesn't belong to you. You will know if it is truly yours, I can assure you. There is no doubt.

Life just catches up with you sometimes. There is an agenda. You have a job, a family, obligations, and responsibilities—things to do, people to see, bills to be paid. It can create a frantic form of stress and anxiety that is always humming away in the background. It reminds me of White Rabbit, the character from the book *Alice in Wonderland*, who's constantly running around looking at his watch, afraid of what the Queen will do to him if he is late. Doesn't it strike you as odd how we are all a little like White Rabbit? We are always afraid we will get into trouble if we don't do something that is expected of us. It is an endless cycle that never seems to end.

I was caught up in that cycle for years. Over time I started to realize that there were two parts to the stress and anxiety I was feeling in my life. One was the responsibility agenda to my family, my career, my employer etc. The other piece was what I was picking up from other people intuitively. Not only was I reacting to my own personal stress, but I was allowing the stress and anxiety that other people were feeling to become my problem too.

"How did that happen?" I wondered.

Looking for answers, I started to analyze and tease apart what was mine and what belonged to other people. Going through that process reduced my anxiety substantially. It really made sense. Everything is connected and it was only natural that I would be able to feel that. Most of us have heard of the analogy of the chaos theory. If a butterfly flaps its wings in North America, it affects the weather in Africa.

I was a drop of water in the ocean. My ego was making me feel separate. My inner calm was reminding me that we are all connected. If you have two tuning forks and you tap one, the other turning fork will begin to hum in unison. Energy moves energy. You are energy and your feelings create energy. It is only logical that any energy you generate will begin to affect the energy around you. Listening to the wisdom my intuition offered helped to remind me that it would only stand to reason that if I am feeling sadness then the person standing next to me is also going to begin to feel sadness.

For the person standing next to me, though, that sudden feeling of sadness could become very confusing, couldn't it? If, for example, Sally is standing beside me and she is unaware that I am feeling sad because I am acting happy, it creates a contradiction to what she is seeing physically (happy) but what she is feeling internally (sadness). This is very confusing for people who are very intuitive but unaware of their intuition. The contradiction between what they are seeing and what they are sensing intuitively can create quite the dilemma.

One reaction would be to just fluff it off as a passing emotion. Or she could start to worry about "feeling sad" and start to wonder why she feels that way. In general, I have found that the most common response would be for her to take ownership of that feeling of sadness and think it was hers. It would cause her some confusion as she begins to analyze her feelings. In order to justify it, her ego would be trying to find an emotional connection as to why she feels that way.

Because she is out of touch with her intuition, she wouldn't be aware of the real truth, which is the fact that she is feeling my sadness.

Let's take this analogy one step further to demonstrate how a simple conversation can create unnecessary stress and anxiety in your life based on how you react to feelings around you.

I am at a party and I strike up a conversation with my friend, who we will call Herb. I mention to Herb that I just finished reading a really great novel, and he says he read it too. We begin to discuss the plot and symbolism of the book in great detail. While I am enjoying this conversation and glad for the distraction, deep down I am feeling sad because I just had an argument with one of my children. I am not happy with how things transpired and I am having a hard time shaking off the sadness. I am feeling sad but pretend to be having a good time anyway. Nobody needs to know what just happened at home, so I am hoping that eventually I can shake off feeling sad about it.

During my conversation with Herb, though, that argument I just had with my child is replaying itself over and over again in the back of my mind. My ego is busy chastising me for the things I said, which only adds to my feelings of sadness. Herb, on the other hand, is completely unaware of what I am really feeling and starts to also feel sadness, and this starts to bother him. He can't understand why he is suddenly feeling sad. He is having this great conversation with me and he is thrilled I just happened to be reading the same book. But that feeling of sadness simply won't go away even after he moves onto another conversation with another person at the party. He starts to think about why he is feeling sad and tries to find an emotional connection. His ego is trying to justify those feelings by finding a reason based on his own personal experiences.

Herb begins to think: "Maybe I feel sad because I shouldn't have made that comment about the author of that book to Atherton? Or maybe I feel sad because I forgot to finish that assignment at work on time and it will really annoy my coworkers. Or maybe I feel sad because of that fight I got into in Grade 3 with my best friend and we never talked to each other again."

On and on it goes inside of Herb's mind. He continues looking for a connection to the feeling of sadness, but he can't nail it down. He finds that he isn't enjoying the party anymore because he can't get his mind off the sadness, and he is uncertain as to why he feels that way. Herb goes home feeling sad and starts to feel that he didn't enjoy the party very much. The party left him feeling anxious and unsure. He feels like he said or did something wrong but he doesn't know for sure if he did or not. That really bothers him.

At no point in Herb's ruminations about feeling sad did he ask himself the one crucial question: "Is this my sadness or is it someone else's sadness?"

If he had asked himself that question, his intuition would have helped him realize that the sadness wasn't his. It would occur to him that the sudden feeling of sadness is probably coming from me because we are having a conversation in close contact. He would be aware that I am not showing sadness and I am not discussing it. At this point he has two choices. He could either show signs of concern and ask me if I am all right, or he could just acknowledge the sadness and send me loving thoughts.

Intuitives can spare themselves a great deal of stress, anxiety, and grief by remembering to ask that simple question. "Is this mine or someone else's?" You will always know if it is yours because of the way your intuition responds to the question. Any thread of doubt means it isn't yours, so let it go in love, and let it be.

6. Be honest

When I am working with clients, I see first-hand how much stress and anxiety is created by being afraid to be honest. You don't want to offend anyone, so it is just easier to play along. This is especially true in situations such as with family obligations, partner's expectations, or invitations from friends when you don't want to go, despite the fact that you know it will make you feel miserable and make you regret how you compromised yourself.

One of the reasons I think this is such a problem is because we have been conditioned to always do as we are told. One of the first things we learn as children is that we have to obey our parents. As we grow up, we are told we need to listen to the teacher, then our employer. Anybody with a title or a degree is viewed as an "authority," and it is expected that they will be listened too. It can get us into trouble sometimes because most of us never learned when it was all right to become our own authority. Not listening and honoring our own authority can place us in situations where we are always acquiescing to other people's wants and needs. We lose our ability to honor our own free will and compromise our integrity in the process. It can also boil down to the simple fact that we just don't know how to say NO. We would rather worry and feel guilty than risk offending someone else. And that adds a lot of additional stress and anxiety to our lives.

There is an art to saying NO and staying true to yourself without offending another person. How a person *chooses* to react is their free will. How you *choose* to say NO is your decision and is an act of free will and choice. You have no control, nor is it your responsibility, to control or manage how other people react. This will help you understand how to develop clear boundaries.

How to Say No

Learning to say NO in a loving and kind way is a talent that can be easily developed. For example, say you have been offered an invitation you don't want to accept. You can respond by saying:

"What a lovely offer. Thank you so much for the invitation. Unfortunately I am unable to make it," or "Thank you so much for thinking of me, but I don't think so. You go ahead and have fun though and tell me all about it when you get back." If you are the recipient of a response like this to an invitation you have offered, be gracious and accept their refusal with respect. They are being clear about their boundaries and you are accepting that with love and understanding.

Honesty in a relationship is also being clear about boundaries. It shows respect for yourself and respect for the other party involved. For example, if you happened to make a mistake, own up to it. Don't make excuses or fluff it off. Look the person straight in the eye and say, "Yes, you are right. I screwed up. I am sorry."

In the early days of my practice a mom had brought her four-year-old daughter to see me. When they both walked into the treatment room, the little girl came to a dead stop and turned to look at me straight in the eye. She said to me, "Are you all right?"

I was pretty stunned. This kid was only four years old. *How could she possibly be that intuitively connected to the emotions around her at such a young age?* I thought. But you know what, that little four-year-old was right. I paused and quickly checked into my energy field, and I wasn't all right. The session that had just finished before her appointment had been extremely intense. The client had had a huge emotional release. I hadn't cleared my energy field or the energy in the room completely. There were still energetic leftovers in the room, and as a result I wasn't grounded or clear enough emotionally.

I looked at this little girl and said, "You know you are right. I am not all right. Can I have five minutes to rebalance?"

The little girl and her mom went back out into the waiting room. I cleared my energy field and rebalanced the room. When I called them back in, the little girl said, "Oh, this is much better. You can work on me now." She immediately jumped up on my massage table and laid down. The mother tried to apologize for her behavior, but I told her, "No, don't apologize. She was being honest and she was right. I needed to hear that."

I knew that if I had tried to be nice and say, "No, I am fine, thank you," that it would have been a lie. This little girl would have never trusted me again and she would never have let me work with her. Her mother on the other hand would have been totally confused on why her child wouldn't come back because she wasn't listening to what her daughter was trying to tell me.

Being honest with someone can be tough. I get that, but in the long run what are the consequences of not being honest? In the end, truth always wins out. Life would be far less painful and stressful, and we would be far less anxious if we just learned to be honest and up front. I also think it is important to understand how to receive honesty and truth from another with grace and understanding.

Grace

If I ask a friend if they would like to go out and they say they would rather not, I accept it with grace. If a client tells me that they don't feel that I am helping them, I accept their truth. I don't make it all about me. And we do that, don't we. If someone doesn't do what we want them to do, we get very emotional about it. Truth and honesty is also about understanding that the world doesn't revolve around you and you alone. People have their reasons. We don't know everything that is going on in their personal lives. They also shouldn't have to explain or defend their reasons to you.

A Word About Advice

One of the best lessons I have ever learned was that advice is just that—advice. It is one person giving you the benefit of their experience. They just want to share their wisdom. They are only trying to spare you the pain that they suffered when they learned something the hard way. Learn to accept it with grace and love. Just because they have given you advice doesn't mean you have to take it. All you need to do is listen and honor the fact that they are trying to help you.

I have learned a few key phrases that go a long way to helping me honor what is right for me when someone is offering me the benefit of their experience.

If someone gives me unsolicited advice, I say, "Thank you so much for that. That is really helpful. I will have to look into that."

Sometimes the advice I was being offered didn't feel right for me intuitively. In those situations I soon found myself beginning to worry about the "what if" scenario. What if they ask why I didn't do what they suggested?

If I choose NOT to follow their advice, I learned to say: "Thank you for your advice. I gave it a try and it didn't work out for me. But I really appreciate your insights."

People just want to be heard. Acknowledge that you have heard them and then take your own counsel. Some advice I have received over the years has been absolutely brilliant and I am so grateful I listened and tried it out. But I have also been given advice that was just wrong and hurtful. In those situations, I found that if I had listened to my intuition, which was warning me that the advice wasn't right, things might have turned out better. I learned over time to walk the middle road with advice. I listen, I respect it, and I allow myself to check in intuitively to see if it is right for me and then choose from there.

Utilizing these six "Intuitive Ethics" will provide you with practical tools that are easy to apply. They will help you to be more aware of how to use your intuition in a healthy way. It will help you to be more compassionate, authentic, and peaceful as you embrace your intuitive gift. This is all part of learning how to dance with the inner calm of the intuitive mind. The next piece of the intuitive dance is understanding the role fear plays in blocking your connection to the inner calm.

4

Fear vs. Intuition

There is a big difference between fear and intuition. Understanding the difference between the two will change how you perceive everything in your life. Understanding what fear really is and what it is not will help you to trust how to use your intuitive insights safely and more effectively. With that trust comes the ability to live a more heart-centered and loving life. Following your intuition means that you are discovering that there is a difference between the *you*, who you think you are, and the *YOU*, who you really are.

All in all there are only two different emotions—love and fear. Every spiritual book you read, regardless of teacher, religion, or philosophy, will say the same thing. All emotions can be reduced to these two basic emotions. When you examine what fear is and what it isn't, you will find that fear feeds the ego. Whereas when you examine love in the same way, you will discover that love feeds the inner calm within you.

It dawned on me that love and fear were like two separate pieces of the whole that I identified with. Yet they seemed to contradict each other. I started to ask myself, "Why is it so much easier to respond to situations from a place of fear?" "Why is it so hard to respond in a loving, calm way?" I wondered if I was missing something as I continued to practice these new steps on the path of self-awareness.

In his book, *The Biology of Belief*, Dr. Bruce Lipton talks about the two primary divisions of the brain—the conscious and subconscious

minds. He refers to the conscious mind as being "the seat of our personal identity," which is the aspect of the mind that creates positive
thoughts. Whereas the subconscious mind is the "repository of stimu-
lus-response tapes derived from instincts and learned experiences. It is
habitual and only replays back what we have learned from the past." He
goes on to say, "When it comes to sheer neurological processing abilities,
the subconscious mind is more than a million times more powerful
than the conscious mind."

In essence, what he is saying is that the subconscious mind runs the
show, and it is one great big tape recorder—a tape recorder that ONLY
records. As it records it doesn't add in any emotional context, beliefs,
or include the backstory of why, and it doesn't discriminate what it is
recording. It just plays back the message in the way that it originally
recorded it.

Childhood Beliefs

When I was being trained in the healing arts, one particular story our
teacher shared with us had a very deep impact on me. We were talking
about fear and why two people, who experience the same trauma at
the same time, can have totally different memories or fears as a result.
He told us the following analogy: Take two boys, both age three, and
place them in a sandbox to play. Then give each child exactly the same
toy to play with at the same time. A stranger comes along, sees the two
boys playing, and decides to grab both toys at the exact same time and
takes them away. How each child responds to that situation will be
totally different. One boy may shrug his shoulders and find another
toy to play with and think nothing more of it. On the contrary, the
other boy may become traumatized by the situation. He may develop
fears and beliefs, such as "You cannot trust strangers," or "people will
take things away from you," or "that he didn't deserve the toy" or "that
he cannot be trusted." It is all based on what impressions each child's
subconscious mind chooses to record at that moment in time when
the toy is taken away. We have no control on how the subconscious
mind chooses to record events. Or do we?

In his book, *Evolve your Brain*, Dr. Joe Dispenza says, "From childhood through young adulthood we are learning and growing from our environment. Then we reach a point in midlife—whether midlife is a genetic natural phenomenon or a learned, environmental effect—in which we certainly have experienced a lot of what life's experiences and emotions have to offer ... We know how to hate and judge another, and more important, we know how to judge ourselves" (298–299).

It can in many ways feel like we have no choice in what we have learned emotionally by the time we reach adulthood. Life is what life has taught us. Each person's experience and emotional reaction will be different. It is how we grow and mature emotionally and spiritually. However, it can also give us a false sense of hopelessness. We can become trapped into falsely believing that we have no choice because of the events from our childhood: an unnecessary fallacy. We *always* have choice. We may not have a very conscious choice as a child, but that does not mean that we cannot exercise conscious choice as an adult to change a preconceived belief. It is an opportunity to change our minds and change our life. There is always hope, never forget that. There is always choice in how you choose to respond. It is easier to change how you react to things now that you know you have that choice.

As discussed earlier in chapter one, the first five years of life are the most important for the emotional development of the subconscious mind as well as for the physical evolution of the child. It is also important for a child's spiritual development. In the first five years of life, a child is slowly separating from the mother's aura energetically. They are learning to react to life the way the parent reacts. If the mother is afraid to let go of the child, then the child knows fear of separation. If the parent is afraid of cats, then the child will grow to fear cats and not understand why. An anxious parent will usually result in an anxious child. Not because the parent is teaching anxiety but because the child sees how the parent responds to life with anxiety. The child's subconscious mind records that belief that this is how you are supposed to respond to life's events, with anxiety. Their belief then becomes embedded with additional experiences without any emotional context or subtext around the "why" the parent acted this way. The child learns to never question why they too react this way.

Dr. Bruce Lipton says that when it came to small children, the Jesuits were aware of this programmable state and proudly boasted, "Give me the child until he is seven and I will give you the man." I see evidence of this in my practice every day. A client will come in suffering from anxiety. Everything makes them anxious and they can't understand why. Their anxiety has been so long term that they are even experiencing physical symptoms of chronic pain that nothing seems to heal. They have done years of therapy, tried medication and mediation, been hospitalized, and even endured exploratory surgery to try and find the source of their physical pain, yet it is still there. When we work together, we inevitably discover a childhood memory that is imprinted on the subconscious mind, which is the "trigger" for a lot of their anxious reactions to life. Find the trigger, change the belief, and the body heals.

Programming Received as Children

Naturally there are situations where the parents had nothing to do with the level of fear or anxiety that children have been exposed to in the early years of their life. One client of mine, Greta, was a prime example of that.

Greta was a very spry octogenarian who eagerly walked into my office with the assistance of two canes one day. Although she suffered from osteoarthritis, was hard of hearing, and had a knee and a hip replacement, she lived alone and was actively involved in her local community. She told me that she suffered from anxiety and she felt sad all the time. Greta had hoped that maybe energy medicine could help her uncover why she was not getting better despite everything she had tried. As we worked together, we uncovered deep-seated fears from her childhood that had become so much a part of her life that she didn't even realize how much they were impacting her.

Greta was a German Jew, born just when Hitler came to power. She told me, "As a child growing up in Germany before World War II, the Jewish community was bombarded with messages that said 'We were no good,' and that worried me because, as a small child, I was afraid it might be true. As a result, all my life I have believed at some level that I am no good."

By the year 1937, it looked like persecution was inevitable. Her father made the critical decision to get his family out of Germany before it was too late. They barely made it out before the borders closed. They lived in relative peace in Belgium until 1942, when the Germans invaded that country. Forced to go into hiding, the family was split up for everyone's safety and sent to live with different families. Greta was sent to live in an apartment with a man and his wife who had no children. She was eleven years old, scared, and separated from her family for the first time in her life. She would not know who in her family had survived until the war ended three years later.

When Greta arrived at her new lodgings she was told that she could never leave the apartment and she must never, under any circumstances, ever look out any of the windows. If anyone suspected that she was there, they were all dead. It was as simple as that. Hidden away for the duration of the war, her greatest fear was that they would all be discovered and killed by the Germans. Keeping her silence was a matter of life or death—for everyone.

That apartment became her prison cell. There was no escape, no one to turn to, and no one to help her. And the man who lived there knew it. It didn't take long before he took advantage of the situation and began his nightly visits.

She didn't know what to do except endure the abuse and keep silent because talking might have meant the end for all of them. So every night for three years she suffered in silence with no one to reach out to.

Using this information about her life story, we started to gently work through Greta's memories. As she recalled the memories of what happened to her during the war, it helped her to understand where the subconscious fear was coming from. As a result of those fears, she understood why she held certain deeply entrenched beliefs that weren't really true for her. Changing those beliefs gave her the opportunity to start living the truth of who she really was. Having this shift in consciousness allowed her body to release the blocks of energy that not only gave her physical pain but emotional sadness and despair.

After several months of working together, Greta came into the office one day and said, "You won't believe it!" She had a huge grin on her face. "My feelings have come back! I am feeling again. 300 percent." For Greta, understanding that her sadness was a result of all the anxiety she had carried with her since the war gave her the ability to feel her emotions and experience joy again. Physically, Greta was thrilled to have more range of movement in her arms and less pain in her hips. Greta, who never believed she would ever find herself again after everything that had happened to her, learned that she is a good person and that she does matter. Greta now sees what a wonderful, loving person she is and is able to live from that new truth. Her sadness and anxiety are gone. Life is beautiful.

This is the power of the subconscious mind.

This is the power of fear.

This is the power of love.

Legitimate Fear vs. Manufactured Fear

If the subconscious mind is just one large tape recorder that dutifully records all of our experiences, it is no wonder that the programming we receive as children growing up is so important. It is also no wonder we have a hard time not living in constant fear.

But there are two types of fear.

There is the fight-or-flight response, which is true and legitimate fear.

If you are out for a walk and a bear starts to charge you, you will run for your life. This is not the time to try to connect to your intuition or try to intuitively talk the bear down. Run! This is true fear. Science refers to it as our built-in defense system that helps to protect us from unknown stimuli. It is a natural part of our survival system.

And there is fear for the sake of being fearful. I call this "manufactured fear."

Our egos do a great job of manufacturing fear. Some of this is totally justifiable. Take Greta for example. She was trapped in a small apartment, with strangers, in the middle of a war. She had no one to help her. Her survival instincts kept her going. She survived. What she endured during the war taught her a level of self-reliance that few of us ever have the opportunity to develop. That was a gift and it helped her to raise a young family on her own. This is the wonder and power of the human spirit. But this experience created fear beliefs in her that also hampered her self-esteem and emotional well-being, which in turn created physical symptoms that were crippling her. They no longer needed to be there.

Greta's story demonstrates that who we really are is not the sum total of our programming. We all experience life in different ways. Well-meaning advice and guidance we receive from our parents and other authority figures only further serves to create additional fear, which can make it very difficult to get in touch with our inner calm. All of this creates different beliefs and realities for each of us.

Now there are legitimate fear factors that must be learned: don't touch a hot stove, don't put a pen into an electrical outlet, don't run out in traffic, look both ways, etc. These are valid forms of fear programming. We can get carried away with the fear, though, and it can create unrealistic expectations and problems for us, both emotionally and physically.

Manufactured fear creates a fight in our minds that we feed and nurture before we decide that the manufactured fear must be the truth. It is the fear based on what you think is true, must be true, or has to be true. It is the illusion your ego wants you to believe. It makes you believe you are separate—alone—when the truth is we are all connected. We are all love. It is the subconscious battle between fear and love that is the root cause of stress and anxiety. We are trying to find the love—truth—but it is blocked by fear—ego.

Stress and anxiety can be killers. It takes its toll physically and emotionally. It is one thing to meet a deadline at work, and it is another to cloak that deadline in fear of things we have created in our minds. We start to think things like: if I don't get this project done in time, I just know I will get fired; I don't have what it takes to get this project done; everyone at work is waiting for me to fail on this project; if only Bob would do his bit then this project would be a success; my husband doesn't understand what I am going thorough to get this project done. Irrational thought-based fears like these are the true motivators of stress and anxiety that can't be resolved just through diet or exercise. It is the type of fear that can only be resolved through inner reflection.

Practicing Self-Reflection

That little voice in the back of your mind keeps creating these fearful thoughts, making things more difficult than they need to be. Let's face it—there are lots of voices in our heads. There is the critical voice, the happy voice, the baby voice, the angry voice, the mother voice, the father voice, the self-incriminating "I told you so" voice. Then there is the voice of love, the voice of compassion, and the voice of understanding and warmth. That is the inner calm voice of your intuition that lets you know that everything will be okay.

How do you know the difference between fear manufactured by the ego and the voice of calm that lets you feel love? It is really very simple. The inner calm voice of your intuition is always calm, peaceful, and it always feels right. It feels true. It feels safe and sure. It is steady, reassuring, and knowing. It is a loving voice.

The ego voice is always anxious, fearful, and doubtful. It uses I, you, we, they, should, have, need, want, got to. It makes you feel guilt, remorse, anger, fear, sadness, despair, helplessness, uselessness, regret, etc. It either makes you feel like you can't do anything right or you are the only person who is right.

If you intuitively feel that something is right, and then you hear "the voice" telling you that you are wrong, then you know you had an intuitive hit and your ego wants to deny it. The inner calm revealed to you by your intuition is showing you the path of love, and the ego is showing you the way of fear. You can choose between the two.

It will take time for you to understand the difference. That is all right. It will happen. All you have to do is decide to give yourself permission to listen to the different tone and language of the inner voices. Then practice listening. The more you listen the easier it becomes to discern between the two and follow your intuition.

I had to learn this practice of self-reflection the hard way. When I was a teenager in high school, it didn't take long for the other kids at school to figure out that Atherton was just a little off plumb as far as they were concerned. For one thing, I was sitting in the lunchroom eating vegetarian meals while reading books on Eastern religions in a Catholic high school. For the first time in my life, the teasing made me feel like I was really different from everyone else. It was painfully clear that I was not being accepted by my peers. I found myself becoming more emotional and insecure. I started to come home from school in the emotional throes of some perceived verbal wrongdoing that created deep angst. Wounded and bruised over something that happened at school, whether it was instigated by me or received as the brunt of an unkind action from someone else, it would have me reduced to a puddle by the time I reached the front door of my home.

There was this really cute guy in my class that I had a serious crush on. One day he walked past me in the hallway and with hope in my eyes, I smiled at him. He stopped and looked at me and told me I was a weirdo. I was devastated. As soon as I got home I ran into the kitchen, tears streaming down my face. My mother was standing at the kitchen counter cutting carrots into little sticks. I stood there crying my heart out and telling her that nobody liked me and I was weird. Finally she turned to me and said, "What do you want me to do about it?"

I hit the roof. I started yelling at her and telling her she didn't understand me and that it was her fault everybody thought I was weird and that she didn't love me. She stood there and looked at me and said, "You are mad because you don't think you fit in. This isn't about me, this is about you and how you feel about yourself. Why don't you go to your room and look into your belly button and figure out why you feel that way about yourself."

And then without another word she quietly turned back to cutting up carrots.

I was furious! I stomped to my room and slammed the door as hard as I could. I fell on my bed and wailed my heart out. After a short period of time, in the throes of all this drama, I became aware of me standing beside the "me" lying on the bed. It was surreal. With curiosity I stood there and watched how her thoughts fed her tears. That's when it dawned on me that I was creating all this fear in my life. I suddenly "saw" how I had manufactured all this fear about not being accepted. I had tried to make it my mother's fault, but she would have none of it. She forced me into looking into my own heart so that I could understand how I created my own fear. Telling me to look into my belly button was her way of showing me how to practice self-reflection.

I used that self-reflection to help me cope with being different from the other kids. It helped me to realize that I wanted to be me, my authentic self, and not be like the herd.

It took me years to understand that my mother was, in her own way, trying to teach me not to be afraid of my manufactured fear created by my ego. By insisting that I "look at my own belly button," she was forcing me into a deeper level of contemplation of my ego voice. It helped me to really "hear" it and understand how manipulative it could be.

Over the years of experiencing many other belly button days, I started to understand that I could use the inner calm of my intuition to observe how my emotions and beliefs were all manufactured based on judgment, assumptions, and reactions from my ego. I started to see how I could buy into what the ego was saying (manufactured fear) or transform what the ego was saying into different beliefs (inner calm). I also started to see that I could challenge my ego and ask, "Why?" but that only happened when I was grounded enough to stay conscious through all the emotional fury and self-made drama manufactured by my ego in the first place. When I was grounded enough, I could see just how much I was actually in control of what happened to me. I started to see how changing my mind changed the experience. It would move me from fear to inner calm.

We always have a choice in the type of experience we have. Whether it is to believe manufactured fear created by the ego or the inner wisdom that our intuition is showing us. We can make it easy or we can make it difficult. We can make it all about ME or we can make it all about THEM. Either way there is a level of responsibility to how we choose to respond.

In my case, I had to take responsibility for my own thoughts and feelings and stop expecting other people around me to be responsible for how I felt about myself. This reduced the level of anxiety I felt, my stress levels came down, and I started to enjoy more periods of feeling calm and peaceful.

We all have that tendency, in my experience, to run away from these rich moments of self-reflection. Instead, we choose to marinate in the manufactured fear and wallow in a pool of depressing feelings that condemn us to powerlessness. I think that if we actually gifted ourselves this quiet time of emotional release, of "being in our belly buttons," we could be much healthier emotionally. It would release us from the suffocating power of a controlling ego and shift us into a more powerful and deeper connection to the inner calm that is our natural birthright.

Belly Button Time

When you are feeling the need for belly button time, find a quiet place to be alone. Get out your journal and some colored pens. Lock the door or go to the bathroom and pour a nice bath. Tell your family that you want some time alone and you are not to be disturbed, or say you want to meditate or that you want to have some "me" time. You are giving yourself permission to be in touch with your feelings.

When you are alone, get in touch with the story and walk into the emotions of what you are feeling. Listen to them. Give yourself permission to cry, sob, and feel sorry for yourself. Allow each emotion to surface and pool around you. Embrace the wound. Wallow in the emotional quagmire that will finally allow the real truth to bubble to the surface. Journal all of your thoughts and feelings. If you are aware of the conflict between your ego voice and your inner calm voice, write out the argument from both sides. Ask how old the pain is. If you find that it is very young in age, hug the inner child and let her rant about the pain. There will come a moment when you will start to see the truth behind the story. As the truth begins to float to the surface, ask yourself, "What was I looking to learn from this?" Recognize the pain, acknowledge the lesson, and embrace the love. And then forgive yourself.

Another useful technique for having belly button time is focusing on your predominant type of intuition. A clairvoyant may find that the belly button technique is the easiest because they can visualize having the experience and watch themselves going through it, like watching a movie. A clairsentient is really going to feel the emotions inside the gut. They will find that writing them out might be the most effective way to do the belly button technique. But make sure what you are feeling is in fact really yours before you spend any precious emotional time processing what you are feeling. If you are clairaudient, you will find that writing down what you hear and then talking it out with yourself to be the most effective. A claircognizant is going to feel this in one of two ways. They will either feel this coming from their heart or they will feel the information flowing down from their crown chakra, at the top of their head. For this reason, they may find that talking, writing, and then allowing themselves to be the observer in combination to be very effective.

I am a big believer in journaling for this reason. It is amazing what you can pull out of your subconscious when you start to write down the things that are upsetting you. I also like to use different colored pens when I am upset. I will use blue for my voice, a red pen for the anger, an orange pen for the ego voice, and a purple pen for my intuitive inner calm voice. Try it. I think you may be pleasantly surprised by what you read.

With experience you may find that journaling and practicing belly button time can help to reveal a pattern of behavior that needs to be re-examined. The mystics teach that we continue to experience the same events, the same cycle of pain, in different ways over and over again until we recognize the pattern and accept the lesson the soul is trying to learn. When you recognize what the lesson is, the pattern never needs to repeat itself.

We cannot truly understand how our subconscious fears have kept us prisoners in our own lives if we are not willing to take the journey into our fears and be the observer. There is so much we can learn from our egos' fears if we have the courage to ask, "Why is this here? Why do I believe this? Is it really true?"

As you become more adept at listening to your intuition, you will find that it becomes easier to recognize what is real and legitimate fear versus the learned, or manufactured, fear. With this new perspective comes more equanimity of mind. There is so much freedom to be gained if you are open to using your intuition to investigate your manufactured fears. Explore the connection between the ego and inner calm. Listen to the manufactured fear. Listen to the inner calm voice. Feel the difference. Understand the difference. You will soon learn how your intuition is guiding you through fear to find the truth of inner calm. With that comes the truth that you are divinely loved and can never be alone.

Part II
Building
Your Energy

Developing your intuitive gifts and understanding the different types of fear and how they control you can go a long way to helping you reduce the stress and anxiety in your life. As you practice exploring the difference between your ego voice and your inner calm voice, you may well begin to notice that life takes on a different perspective.

The next step to learning how to deal with this newfound information about who and what you are energetically is exploring how to manage your energy more effectively. There are a few simple techniques that you can learn very quickly that will help you achieve that. The first is learning how to be more grounded and present. The next technique is learning what happens to your energy while you sleep and how you can manage getting a deeper, more restful sleep that will help you wake up feeling restored and ready for a new day. Lastly, there is the art of learning how you manifest what you want in life while undoing the false illusions created by your old ego belief systems.

5

Grounding to Stay Calm, Cool, and Collected

Have you ever had one of those days where everything felt off? You feel emotional, discombobulated, frazzled, agitated, and miserable. You can't find things. You can't remember where you put the car keys, or you try to put the milk in the cupboard. You suddenly find yourself trying to put the dog in the closet instead of out the door. You know, one of THOSE days!

We all have them. They are frustrating and annoying. It can bring you to tears in the blink of an eye. You can find yourself blowing up over silly little things that really don't mean anything in the grand scheme of life. You want to rant at anybody, everybody, and everything in your life. It takes your already stressed out life and racks it up a few more notches, and you start to wonder if the weekend will ever get here. My mother used to refer to these days as feeling "all sixes and sevens."

I didn't like those days. When they happened to me I would flounder at work or around the house. Nothing seemed to get done and I felt like I was running around in circles. I found myself making silly mistakes or bad decisions that only brought more unhappiness, regret, and guilt. I became moody, irritable, and unhappy. Then, just when I was at the apex of feeling like my life was falling apart and I was scared of becoming depressed, I learned about grounding. I realized that when I was having one of THOSE days, I wasn't grounded. Suddenly feeling off and all sixes and sevens wasn't threatening anymore. What a relief it was to discover I could actually do something about it.

I also learned that not being grounded meant that my energy field, or aura, was off kilter and it was trying to correct itself and come back to the center. As I learned more about my intuitive abilities, I realized that I was also picking up other people's energy and carrying it in my energy field. It didn't need to be there, and the only way I could clear my energy field was to either cry or get angry. In essence, I was short-circuiting and needed to clear the static so that my body could make itself right again. That made sense to me. If everything is energy and I am energy and the energy isn't flowing smoothly, then of course I would feel all sixes and sevens!

Learning to Ground

Life is already busy enough with responsibilities to our families, jobs, etc. Being ungrounded only adds a lot of additional and unnecessary stress and anxiety to our lives. What if there was a way to stay grounded and clear-headed even when everything around you seems to be out of control and senseless? I learned that there was a very powerful yet simple technique that would have me feeling totally grounded, and it takes just a few minutes a day. It is called the Vertical Axis.

When I did the Vertical Axis consistently, the easier life became. I found this simple technique helped to keep my wits about me, even in the middle of a crisis. I was being less reactive. When I went to bed at night, I noticed that I would fall asleep faster. That was a bonus. My mind became quieter. That was a relief. If something upset me, I could calm down faster and think more rationally. My ability to manifest what I wanted became easier and more frequent. It was easier to meditate. I felt more connected to life.

I learned that when you are grounded, you are less likely to be influenced by other people's wills and private agendas. You are more aware and in control emotionally, mentally, and physically. Daily practice of the Vertical Axis made meditation easier, and I found that I was feeling a deeper sense of inner peace. It helped me to feel more spiritually connected and peaceful. My sense of purpose felt stronger and more obtainable. I started to know and understand that if I felt emotional about something, I could determine if it was mine or someone else's. If it wasn't mine, then I could release the energy and not be affected by it. This dynamic and very powerful technique was like no other grounding technique I had ever tried before. I started to look forward to doing it every day and could tell when I had forgotten to do it just by how my day transpired. Doing the Vertical Axis has since become part of my daily morning ritual.

Various Forms of Grounding

When I first began to learn about grounding, teachers would tell me that it meant having your feet firmly planted on the land and feeling part of Mother Earth. That made sense to me. My mother would often have us take off our shoes and go outside to play when we were small. During the summer when we lived at our cottage, we were encouraged to run around shoeless all the time, regardless of the weather. Every night, after running around all day without our shoes on, my mother would fill a bucket with warm soapy water and we would sit in front of the wood stove and wash all the dirt and tar from our feet. We loved it. If we were feeling miserable, she would tell us to, "Go outside and feel the grass under your feet. Smell the earth. That will calm you down." And she was right, it did.

Teachers would have me use that memory from my childhood to remind me what being grounded felt like. In the beginning this memory of sitting on the grass in my bare feet felt wonderful. But after a short time I noticed that it wasn't enough. I couldn't understand why. It wouldn't take much to happen at work or in my personal life to throw me off again. It was frustrating.

Then someone taught me that having a bath or shower was very grounding. Well, having a bath was one of my favorite things to do in life. It helped when I was really upset and needed a time out, but again I found the effects were only temporary. I felt like I was missing the big picture because it wouldn't hold for any length of time.

Another grounding technique that I was told to try was sleeping. That also made sense to me. Anytime I had been upset or unsure of how to solve a problem, it would be suggested that I sleep on it. "You will feel better in the morning," is a common expression, after all. Well, I slept A LOT! Next to a hot bath, having a nap or sleeping in was one of my most favorite things in the whole world. But still, in the grand scheme of things in my life, I was not what anyone would have regarded as being well-grounded. If you are a poor sleeper or need to take sleeping pills to sleep, this type of grounding method is hardly of any use at all.

It was surprising to learn that eating was considered to be quite grounding. Everybody has their comfort food, and food is often one of the first things that most people will turn to if they are upset. How often have you turned to your favorite comfort food when you were upset about something happening in your life? I know I have. And let's face it, being told to go eat something so you can be more grounded sounds like a fun thing to do. However, I didn't find it to be a very practical approach to solving my own problems.

Well-meaning friends tried to explain to me that exercising and having a massage would also help me become more grounded. I tried both, but it wasn't helping me either. It wasn't carrying me through the day.

Each person or teacher that I met would share how they grounded themselves. I tried them all. Some worked for a little while, but other techniques made no sense to me, so I didn't bother. I felt frustrated and discouraged because I was aware of the simple fact that there is the day-to-day reality of living.

When life was too busy and stressful, or I was feeling anxious, overwhelmed, and scared, taking time to slip out to take a walk, have a nap, or get something to eat wasn't a very practical approach to grounding myself. Instinctively, I knew that I needed something more. I needed something that would help keep me centered throughout the day. The Vertical Axis changed all of that for me. It was a quick and easy way to do it, and most importantly, it held.

An Overview of the Vertical Axis Technique

What makes the Vertical Axis[2] such a solid, vibrant grounding technique? It is the fact that it teaches you how to ground into nature and the Divine at the same time. When you are connected to heaven and earth at the same time, the two life energies combine together to form a channel of energy that is called the Vertical Axis.

Grounding into the Vertical Axis will help you to clear mental chatter, calm the mind, manage fear, reduce stress and anxiety, make decisions more easily, create a firm foundation for meditation, and allow you to follow your intuition more easily. When you are connected to this energy, you feel calmer, more peaceful, and you have a deeper sense of empowerment. This is where you begin to just "know" and understand that you cannot change the way others react, but you can manage how you react.

I originally learned the Vertical Axis technique from Andrea Mathieson, who is the creator of a line of nature-based essences called the Raven Essences. Andrea has very graciously given me permission to share this amazing technique with you.

She teaches that when we ground or connect with our vertical axis, we are accessing two important sources of energy. The first is our connection to the Divine, or Spiritual Intelligence, which is our soul connection to heaven, not just to our higher self but also to the universal life source of our spirit or soul.

The second is the connection to the Intelligence of Nature, which is our connection to the soul of Mother Earth. By connecting to both at the same time, it is a more stable form of grounding.

Grounding into the Intelligence of Nature is slightly different than grounding into Mother Earth and not quite what you expect. This is because grounding into the Intelligence of Nature and grounding into Mother Earth are two totally separate things.

---

2. The original technique was created by Therese Conway-Killan with Andrea Mathieson of Raven Essences: *http://ravenessences.com*.

Originally we were taught that to ground into Mother Earth we needed to connect to her core. But because she is undergoing too many changes at this time, Mother Earth has requested we no longer connect to her core. Instead we are asked to connect to the Intelligence of Nature, which is responsible for creating Mother Earth. By grounding into the Intelligence of Nature, you are grounding into the soul of what created our earth. It has become more stable at this time.

As you learn the Vertical Axis technique, you may feel like you are making this all up. That's okay. Go ahead and pretend. Form always follows thought. It is what manifesting is all about. In this technique you will be asked to follow three steps. The first step will be imagining or pretending that you have roots coming out of the base of your tailbone (or spine) and feet. As your roots come down out of your tailbone, you will imagine or pretend that they quickly and easily penetrate deep into the earth and that they feel strong, stable, and secure. Your roots will be flexible and can quickly and easily penetrate any surface, no matter what surface they have to go through. You will then imagine that your roots are drawing up the energy from the Intelligence of Nature quickly and easily, and it will feel like drawing water up through a straw.

The second step will be to imagine or pretend that you can see up through the top of your head and up to the blue sky. Then sense and feel a beam of light coming down from the heavens and into your body. This energy will come down from the heavens like a sunbeam and feel like warm sunlight touching the top of your head. You will then imagine that you are able to draw this energy of Spiritual Intelligence down into your body. Feel it going into every cell of your body quickly and easily.

The third step will be to imagine that you are present inside your heart. Here you will sense and feel the combined energy of the Intelligence of Nature and Spiritual Intelligence swirling and dancing together like sunlight dances on the water.

As you go through the Vertical Axis, you may feel the energy, imagine the energy, or sense the energy. For some there may be concern that you are not feeling anything at all. Not to worry. Your body is getting it even if you think you can't feel it. You will still reap the benefits either way. Again, if at any time you feel like you are making this all up, that is all right; you go right ahead and pretend because form always follows thought.

Doing the Vertical Axis will take about five to ten minutes the first few times you practice it. After you have done the technique two or three times, you will find that you can do the entire technique in less than two minutes. You may also find it surprising just how often solutions to problems will come to you after connecting to your vertical axis.

I recommend doing the Vertical Axis twice a day, once in the morning before you begin your day and again in the evening to finish your day. In the mornings, it will help you stay centered and more focused throughout the day. In the evenings, you will find that doing the Vertical Axis will help you to sleep more deeply and wake up feeling more restful. Eventually you will find that doing the Vertical Axis is like exercising a muscle and will become a natural part of your daily routine.

❧ Technique ❧
The Vertical Axis Technique, Step-by-Step

Make yourself comfortable. You can sit up or lie down. Have your journal and pen ready in case you would like to make notes after you are done—sometimes answers to problems suddenly reveal themselves after completing this technique. If you feel like you are imagining or pretending while doing this technique, that if fine. Go ahead and make it up. Form always follows thought. This technique should not be done while driving or operating machinery.

Sitting up with your feet flat on the floor or lying down in a comfortable position, begin to take slow, deep breaths.

Feel your breath going deeply into your belly, and slowly release each breath out.

Feel the ease with which your chest rises and falls with each breath.

As you exhale, allow all the tension in your muscles to release.

Take a few more slow, deep breaths.

With each breath, sense the tension streaming out of your body as all your muscles relax.

Feel yourself relaxing.

Take a few more slow, deep breaths.

Now turn your attention to your tailbone or the base of your spine.

Imagine or pretend that there is a root moving down from your tailbone and down into the earth.

As this root goes down into the earth, imagine or pretend that there are also roots forming at the base of your feet.

Feel how easily all these roots can penetrate the ground. They travel through any surface, quickly and easily.

They go deep, deep down into the earth quickly and easily.

If you feel like you're making this all up—go ahead—imagine it. Pretend it. Your body is getting it.

Now imagine or pretend you can feel the richness of the earth—smell the earth. Feel the roots going deep into the earth, like a tree rooting itself deep, deep, deep into the earth. Feel your roots spreading out for miles and miles anchoring you deep into the earth.

Continue to breathe slowly and easily.

Pause here. Now ask to connect to the Intelligence of Nature. As you make the request, you immediately begin to feel the energy of the Intelligence of Nature moving up into your roots. Imagine that this energy from the Intelligence of Nature is like water and your roots are drawing it up into your body. It feels like water moving up through a straw. As you breathe in, feel the Intelligence of Nature gently and easily moving up into your feet, legs, thighs, abdomen, and chest.

Feel the energy of the Intelligence of Nature moving up into your heart. Hold it here in your heart for a few moments. Feel the energy of it, breathe it in, and relax into it. Feel how it nurtures you. Feel how it feeds you energetically.

Feel the energy of the Intelligence of Nature moving up your chest. Feel how it flows down into your arms, up into your neck, and into your head.

As the energy of the Intelligence of Nature fills your head, imagine that the top of your head is opening up like a flower. Feel the energy flowing down over your body like water in a fountain.

As the energy from the Intelligence of Nature flows over you, feel it washing away all the tension in your body. Feel it washing away all your anxiety, fears, and worries.

Feel yourself connect to the love and warmth of the Intelligence of Nature. Become one with the energy flow. Feel how the Intelligence of Nature is washing and cleaning your energy field. Pause here for a few moments.

Breathe slowly and deeply.

Now turn your attention back to the top of your head. Imagine that you can see up through the top of your head. As you look up through the top of your head, imagine that you are looking up at the heavens.

As you look up at the clear blue sky of the heavens, ask to be connected to Spiritual Intelligence.

As you make the request, imagine that a beautiful white beam of light immediately comes down from the heavens and enters through the top of your head. Feel the energy of Spiritual Intelligence running down into your head. It feels warm like sunlight.

Let the energy of the Spiritual Intelligence run down through your head and into your throat, down into your arms and shoulders, and down into your heart.

Allow yourself to feel the warmth of the energy from the Spiritual Intelligence inside your heart. It feels warm like the sun on your face. Hold the energy of the Spiritual Intelligence here in your heart for a moment. Feel the love of the Spiritual Intelligence and how it fills your heart.

Now take another slow, deep breath and allow the energy of the Spiritual Intelligence to move out from your heart and down into your belly.

Feel the warmth and love of the Spiritual Intelligence moving down into your abdomen, down into your hips, your legs, and then down and out through your feet.

Feel the energy of Spiritual Intelligence moving down into your roots and feel the energy flowing into your roots and flowing out into the earth.

Now bring your attention back into your heart. Imagine that you are inside your heart. Feel and sense the energy of the Intelligence of Nature flowing up from your roots. Feel and sense the energy of Spiritual Intelligence flowing down from the heavens.

Now imagine that the two energies are coming together inside your heart in a dance of love and light. As the two energies come together, it looks like sunlight dancing on the water.

As the two energies come together, feel the love of the intelligence of Nature and the love of Spiritual Intelligence. Feel how the two energies surround you, love you, caress you, and hold you safe. Feel your connection to heaven and earth.

Breathe it in. Take slow, deep breaths. Feel yourself being present in the love.

This is being connected to heaven and earth.

This is being connected to the energy of the Vertical Axis.

Now imagine or pretend that your heart is opening up and all that energy of the Vertical Axis is moving out of your heart and into your entire aura.

Feel the energy of the Vertical Axis filling up all the space around you.

Feel the energy of the Vertical Axis moving out into your home or office.

Feel the energy of the Vertical Axis moving out to your family.

Feel the energy of the Vertical Axis moving out into your town and community.

Now imagine that this energy of the Vertical Axis is moving out and surrounding the entire planet.

Sit quietly for a few moments relaxing into this state of love, light, and balance.

Feel the power of being connected to heaven and earth through the Vertical Axis.

This is being in touch with the God within you and the God that surrounds you.

Feel the love, be the love.

Now imagine all this love coming back to you in gratitude. Let it surround you, hold you, and love you. Breathe, smile, and relax.

When you are ready, slowly open your eyes and breathe deeply, knowing the energy of the Vertical Axis is with you throughout the day.

Once you have learned how to do the Vertical Axis, it is helpful to know that you can hold the energy all day without consciously thinking of it. Just know it to be so.

🪷 Technique 🪷
The Vertical Axis Using Only One Word

As we all know, life can be a challenge sometimes, and it can throw us out of balance when we least expect it. There is a quick way to reconnect to your Vertical Axis at a moment's notice. It is called the One-Word Vertical Axis" technique.

If you suddenly find yourself feeling ungrounded, stressed, anxious, or in a crisis, all you have to do is say your one word and this will reconnect you instantly.

This one-word connection is just as powerful as the full Vertical Axis technique. Your one word can be anything. It can be one word or two words, like peanut butter. It can be a color or an image, like a heart, or a favorite flower. It could be a child's name or a beloved pet's name. The goal is to remain open to receiving what you get without judgment.

To discover your one word for the Vertical Axis:

Make yourself comfortable. You can sit up or lie down. Have your journal and pen ready in case you would like to make notes after you are done—sometimes answers to problems suddenly reveal themselves after completing this technique. If you feel like you are imagining or pretending while doing this technique, that if fine. Go ahead and make it up. Form always follows thought.

> Go into your Vertical Axis outlined on page 93.
> When you are in your Vertical Axis and feeling connected to heaven and earth, ask the universal energy of the Vertical Axis to gift you one word that will take you into your Vertical Axis at a moment's notice.
> Breathe, and let the word come to you. Know that whatever your first impression is, it is your gifted word.
> Write it down
> When you are ready, slowly open your eyes and breathe deeply, knowing the energy of the Vertical Axis is with you throughout the day.

Once you have your one word, you can use it as often or as little as you need it. You don't need to say it out loud. When I use my one word, I say it to myself inside my mind. Learn to use it whenever things feel like they are going sideways or you are in a crisis, and it will quickly and easily bring you back to center.

I use this technique frequently. It has helped me to stay cool, calm, and collected in some pretty dramatic situations. When my mother was dying of a brain tumor, things got very crazy, very quickly. I had to make a lot of painful decisions in a very short period of time. Knowing how to stay grounded while fielding my way through this emotionally complicated time in my life helped me to stay focused, be clear about my emotional boundaries, and do what needed to be done.

After you have used your one word for a while, you may feel that you would like to change it. To do this, go into the full Vertical Axis technique and ask the universe for a new word.

🪷 Technique 🪷
Using the Vertical Axis to Clear Your Energy Field

Once you have learned the Vertical Axis Technique and feel comfortable with the process, you can use the energy of the Vertical Axis to clear your energy field or aura of any negative or ungrounded energy that you may have picked up or been exposed to during the day. I find this particularly helpful after I have been out in crowds or after seeing clients all day. If you are particularly sensitive to other people's feelings and energy, then you will find this technique extremely useful.

Sitting up with your feet flat on the floor or lying down in a comfortable position, begin to take slow, deep breaths.

Go into your Vertical Axis outlined on page 93, or use your one word as outlined on page 97.

> *Feeling the energy of the Vertical Axis and being connected to heaven and earth*
>
> *Feel your breath going deeply into your belly, and slowly release each breath out.*
>
> *Feel the ease with which your chest rises and falls with each breath.*
>
> *As you exhale, allow all the tension in your muscles to release. Take a few more slow, deep breaths.*
>
> *Now ask the energy of the Vertical Axis to clear your field of all negative and ungrounded energy.*
>
> *Imagine that the energy of the Vertical Axis is washing through your energy field and through your entire body, from top to bottom. Feel it moving through all your organs, tissues, skin, cells, and feel it washing away all ungrounded and negative energy.*
>
> *Feel the energy of the Vertical Axis as it is moving out into your entire energy field or aura, and feel it clear away any cloudy, dark energy that may be present there.*
>
> *Imagine that the energy of the Vertical Axis is like water washing you inside and out.*

Feel all the negative and ungrounded energy flowing into the ground, and ask that it be transformed into love and light for the good of all.

See your body and energy field as clear, bright, and flowing freely.

When you are ready, slowly open your eyes and breathe deeply, knowing the energy of the Vertical Axis will stay with you throughout the day and your aura is clear and balanced.

When you are done, thank the energy of the Vertical Axis for its assistance and for transforming all the energy that was released into love and light for the good of all.

Thank the universe for its love and support.

Take another deep breath, wiggle your fingers and toes, and then begin to slowly move around.

I am often asked why we request that any energy being released be transformed into love and light for the good of all. Over the years that I have taught this technique, very sensitive people or empathic children will tell me that they are sometimes afraid to let go of the energy they have picked up from others. They are afraid that if they let it go it will go back to that person or pet and they will be harmed. Helping them to understand that they can safely release this negative energy and request that it be transformed into love and light for the good of all, and how that will benefit the whole universe, has been a huge relief for them. In the process they also learn that they can control what they pick up energetically and how to release it.

Using the energy of the Vertical Axis has become one of the most powerful energy management techniques I have ever learned. I teach it to all of my clients and students. They too have discovered how powerful it is. Learning the Vertical Axis also taught me just how responsible we are for managing what we create in our own lives. Being grounded reminds you that you are safe and loved, and all things are possible. It gives you a firm grasp on how you can let go of old patterns that no longer serve you while opening up the possibilities of creating new internal thought patterns that are healthier and more effective. As Andrea Mathieson has so eloquently said, "You are a soul that has built a body, not a body seeking its spirit!" (2003, 103).

As I practiced the Vertical Axis daily, I began to notice that there were moments during the day when I would suddenly feel these waves of love pour over me. They have since become daily occurrences. When they happen I pause and revel in the love I feel radiating through me. Practicing the Vertical Axis has finally helped me to feel like I can really breathe for the first time in my life. I started to slow down and adjust my priorities. I am becoming more content with the simple things in life. It has made it easier to access my intuition. I know that the challenges with my ego will continue, but I am finding the journey less tedious and time consuming. Hanging out with the inner calm is much more preferable and desirable. The most radical change though has been how much it has reduced not only my stress and anxiety but those of my clients as well. It is my hope that you too will find the inner calm within as you become grounded in your Vertical Axis and enjoy staying cool, calm, and collected. As the Vertical Axis became a regular part of my daily routine, I found doing it at bedtime was giving me a better quality of sleep. I was falling asleep more quickly and waking up with more energy. Then I learned something new that can happen when we sleep. It explained why restful sleep can be so difficult to achieve. The quality of our sleep can be affected by how we dream.

6

Getting Quality Sleep

I think we often lose sight of how important it is to sleep. Instead we see sleep as something that needs to be achieved in as little time as possible so we can work longer, harder hours when we are awake. The days begin to bleed together in a fog of fatigue and anxiety, leaving you feeling hopeless and vulnerable to the challenges in life. As a result, the hope of sleep can develop into an elusive desire, a coveted outcome that never seems to manifest. It is a sad reflection on our sense of what it means for self-care.

Maybe you are one of those people who lie awake at night hoping for sleep, tossing and turning, only to wake up in the morning feeling exhausted. There is nothing harder than being dog-tired and dragging your feet all day, only to have sleep elude you because you can't turn off your mind. It is beyond frustrating to have your ego voice nattering away at you while it delivers a replay of your entire day and provides withering comments and demeaning subtext on every encounter you had. Maddening, isn't it?

What if there was a way to stop that from happening? What if it only took a few minutes to learn how to have a restful night sleep? What if it was really that easy? Do you think you would find it useful? I know I did. It surprised me at how easy it was to change how I slept at night so that I could slow down the monkey mind, drift into a deeply restorative sleep, and wake up feeling refreshed and restored. To help you understand how this works, let's take a look at what happens when we sleep.

When We Sleep

The quality of our sleep has a direct impact on how we function the next day. If we have had a restful night, then our day is productive. On the contrary, the type of day we have had can affect the quality and quantity of sleep we get. How much stress and anxiety we experience affects not only our daytime life but also our nighttime rest.

Stress and anxiety create chemical changes in our bodies that effect how well our body can relax and move into deep, restful sleep. It triggers the production of cortisol, which is the fight-or-flight response hormone produced by the adrenals. When the adrenals are activated, it puts the body on high alert and your body becomes tense. This can affect your sleep cycle because the hormone created by the adrenals, cortisol, will influence the production of melatonin. This hormone is produced by a very small gland buried deep within our brains called the pineal gland.

This gland is actually a very tiny electromagnetic sensor that has a very big job (Dale, 61). Not only does this minute gland regulate our sleep and wake cycle, but it also regulates our moods and intuitive abilities—our innate sense of understanding the things going on around us. The pineal gland, linked to the seventh chakra or higher consciousness, is also associated with our kundalini energy. This energy flows up through the spine from the tailbone into the brain and back down again. The kundalini energy is an important part of our connection to the divine forces of life.

It stands to reason then that if you are unable to silence your mind, then your body cannot relax because it is responding to the emotional threats being manufactured by your ego. This means that thoughts can trigger a fight-or-flight response. If our thoughts can trigger a fight-or-flight response by what we are thinking, it can also be triggered by what is happening as a result of our dreams. Sleep researchers who were studying the brain with the electroencephalogram (EEG), which records brain waves and activity, discovered that everyone does in fact dream. The EEGs demonstrated that we have cycles of sleep and when we enter into a phase called rapid eye movement, or REM sleep, we are actually dreaming. They verified this fact by waking subjects up during a REM cycle and confirming that subjects could remember the dream they were having at the time ("Sleep and Dream: Disorders").

The Physical Side of Sleep

How you take care of yourself at night is just as important as how you take care of yourself during the day. You eat right and exercise, but setting the stage for a restful night is also important. A bedroom should be comfortable, warm, welcoming, and cozy—a sanctuary. The bedroom's only purpose is for rest, relaxation, and sex. Your mattress should be the perfect one for you, and the room should be decorated in soft colors with bedding you adore snuggling into. Bedrooms shouldn't be used for homework or set up as an office during the daytime. If space is limited and it is the only room for your office, use a cabinet designed to hide everything. The room should also be as technologically free of devices as possible. Place cell phones outside the door and try to keep clocks, baby monitors, and sleep apnea machines as far away from your head as possible. If possible, remove the TV to another room so you won't be tempted to watch TV all night. The temperature in the room should also be comfortable with good airflow and a fan or heater, if necessary. Setting a regular bedtime routine is also important to helping you achieve a more restful sleep. Keep a glass of water and a journal and pen at your bedside to record your dreams.

When we are sleeping, we are giving our body a chance to physically restore, repair, and recharge. If we are having trouble sleeping or haven't had a good rest for a long time, we can quickly become sick because the physical body is not getting what it needs to replenish itself. Think of a car running on empty—it just doesn't work. Getting enough rest is important for our physical and mental health because it refills our gas tank.

The truth is: when you deprive your body of deep, restful sleep for long enough, sooner or later your body will become desperate for sleep, and it will try to make up for the deprivation by finding a way to shut off. An example of this would be becoming sick with a cold or flu that knocks you off your feet. If you continue to do it long enough and with enough dedication, you will soon find yourself on stress leave or suffering from a more chronic health condition. However, there is more to getting enough restorative sleep than what happens at the physical level.

Sleep Insight from a Spiritual Perspective

Jewish mystics taught that sleep was not only critical to physical well-being but that it could also have a profound effect on our spiritual growth. They taught that when we sleep we are not only allowing our bodies to heal and restore at a cellular level, but we are also being given the opportunity to repair, heal, and advance at a spiritual level. Some call it doing "soul work" in the dreamtime.

Jonathan Sharp, in his book on *Divining Your Dreams,* states that "the Kabbalists and Jewish mystics have always believed that sleeping and dreaming plays a vital role in our lives" (2002). Jewish mystics have never treated sleep as a waste of time but see it as a very necessary component to not only physical rest but to spiritual purpose. Sharp goes on to write that Hasidic masters (a Jewish movement that came out of Eastern Europe) taught that "No matter how strongly we may feel the need to busy ourselves in activity, time is needed for respite. Without it, we will quickly begin to lose our inner powers."

Different Kinds of Dreams

When we sleep, we dream. Whether you remember your dreams or not, this process is still happening. We all dream but not all of us remember our dreams. Some people remember their dreams occasionally but not all the time. Some people will say they never dream. They do, they just don't remember.

Dreams and lucid dreams can have detailed storylines that seem to go on forever, or they can be so accurate in their details that they depict a future event that comes true. Dreams can be downright bizarre with no rhyme or reason to them. Dreams can be so tense that you wake up filled with anxiety and crying. They can even be so tense that you wake up with aching muscles. For some, dreams turn into nightmares that never seem to end. Others find that their dreamtime is really quite bizarre with radically vivid dreams that can leave them euphoric one day or emotionally devastated the next. Others have an easier time with sporadic nights of on-and-off dreaming cycles.

Other people will tell you that their dreaming is so vivid that it's like they are really there. They feel awake but know that they are sleeping. This is called a "waking dream" or "lucid dreaming." Charlie Morley, in his book *Dreams of Awakening*, states, "A lucid dream is a dream in which we are actively aware that we are dreaming as the dream is happening" (2013, 3). Other mystic teachings, such as those followed by the Sufis, actively encourage their followers to learn lucid dreaming, which is a technique that allows the follower to work consciously in the astral plane during sleep.

Traveling While You Sleep

Would you be surprised to learn that when you go to sleep you actually leave your physical body temporarily and travel into what is called the astral plane? When you are in the astral plane, you dream. Dreams are memories of what we have experienced on the astral plane.

The astral plane is indeed a real place. Theosophy and many other Eastern belief systems have described it in great detail in their sacred documents, which date back thousands of years. C. W. Leadbeater, a leading Theosophy teacher, stated that, "The objects and inhabitants of the astral plane are real in exactly the same way as our own bodies, our furniture, our houses or monuments are real" (1996, 2).

When we are moving through the astral plane, we encounter a world we generally don't consciously understand. It takes years of practice and concentrated study to actually understand it and learn how to move through it in conscious, healthy ways. Most of us don't have the time or inclination to learn that, and it's likely that all you are really interested in is how to get a good night's sleep and manage turning off your monkey mind.

There are two basic levels to the astral plane: the lower astral plane and the upper astral plane. The lower plane is where all the crazy, goofy stuff happens. If your dreams are kooky, don't make any sense, or feel like a nightmare, then you are in the *lower astral plane*. This is the region of the astral plane where you can dream about a dog walking into a bar and ordering a drink for himself with a duck sitting beside him. It is also the area where we will try to help others with their problems or try to work out our own emotional conflicts with others. This is the region of the astral plane where most of us hang out in the dreamtime.

Dreaming in the lower astral plane can be quite confusing because of the way things are seen and experienced. Remember the astral plane is a real place, but it is experienced in a different way because it is entirely energetic. It is best described as being inside a living hologram. In a hologram you experience all dimensions at the same time. For example, if you look at your hand in the astral realm, you can also look through your hand and see the other side at the same time. You can see the front, back, and inside of your hand all at the same time. Numbers can appear as 1818 or 8181. It is very confusing and disorienting. This is also why dreams can be so difficult to understand and interpret. When you are in the astral plane, you can be the person acting out a role in a play, the director of the play, the lighting director, and the audience and all the different characters in the play, all at the same time.

Most people, especially those who are in any type of service industry, have a habit of working very hard all day, so much so that they don't realize they also work very hard in the dreamtime. What does this mean? It means that they work hard all day, go home, go to bed, travel into the lower astral plane, and pick up where they left off at work. They end up working all night trying to make up for the things they feel didn't go as planned during the day. Or they will use this time in the lower astral field to seek out other troubled people or situations and try to help them find solutions. How confusing is that?

The upper astral plane, on the other hand, is where we can problem-solve and seek answers to our life issues. It is here that we can receive spiritual instruction and get help and direction from angels, God, as-cended masters, or guides. In the upper astral plane we can try out different scenarios of future events. We can try out different outcomes or ideas, play out life scenarios, or test the waters, so to speak, on what will happen tomorrow. Sometimes we remember this type of spiritual work when we are awake. We call it a déjà vu. What is important to understand here is that you can enter into the upper astral plane any time you want. All you have to do is remember to ask.

How do you know what part of the astral plane you are visiting? It is really quite simple. Ask yourself if you wake up every morning feel-ing exhausted or if you wake up feeling like you have been struggling with someone or something all night. Do you wake up tense, angry, and irritable and just want to be left alone until you've had a chance to wake up? If you said yes to any of the above, then congratulations— you just spent all night in the lower astral plane either trying to help yourself or save the world.

If you are a particularly empathic or compassionate person with a huge heart, chances are you feel it is your mission in life to help others. This is wonderful, but if you are waking up exhausted and feeling worn out all the time, you begin to wonder how you will ever contin-ue. You may even find that you start to crave privacy and look for ways to retreat from the world because you just can't take it anymore. That can lead to a lot of unnecessary guilt and frustration. Even people who have the most amazing job in the world, where they are truly being of service to others and humanity, can begin to wake up feeling exhaust-ed and drained after a while. It becomes confusing. You feel it is your mission in life to be of service to others, and if you haven't been able to help enough people during the day, then why should you let some-thing as trivial as sleep stand in your way to being of service? And so you start to use the dreamtime as a way to finish what you started in the daytime. Admirable—but in the long term, debilitating.

So how do you move up to the more restful area in the astral world of the dreamtime?

Why Dreamtime Management Is Important

Giving yourself permission to travel to the higher realms of spiritual instruction while you sleep is caring for oneself at an energetic level. It is giving yourself permission to sleep deeply so that the *physical* body can be restored, repaired, and replenished, while at the same time you are restoring, repairing, and replenishing your *energy* body at the mental, emotional, and spiritual level.

I learned all about this the hard way. I am a little service worker bee. When I first opened my healing practice fifteen years ago, I became very busy, very quickly. I was seeing far too many clients each week. I started waking up in the mornings totally exhausted. I had to start taking more and more time off just to recharge. I started to spend less time with my family and I had pretty much stopped talking to friends. It was all I could do to manage my practice and have some sort of a life with my family. Something had to give and I was worried that I was going to have to close my practice.

In sheer desperation I prayed earnestly for help from my angel guardians. I asked them if they could help me be of "right and true service and yet still wake up fully rested."

That night I had a dream that I woke up and could hear all these voices whispering outside my bedroom door. I tentatively got out of my bed and with great caution and trepidation I crept up to the bedroom door and slowly opened it. Much to my absolute shock, there standing before me were all of my clients who had appointments the next day. Immediately a wave of exhaustion overcame me. I was completely overwhelmed. At that moment all of my clients saw me and came rushing over to me. They all started talking to me at the same time. They were all saying, "When I come for my appointment tomorrow, we need to look at this or that." I was flabbergasted. I turned to my Archangel Michael and said in desperation, "What do I do?"

He explained to me that in my need and desire to be of service, I was doing just what I saw here in front of me energetically. Day in and day out I was being of service to others, and then when I slept, I travelled into the lower realms of the astral plane and continued to work with clients, night in and night out.

Archangel Michael said to me, "You don't need to do that. It was not what the universe intended."

I learned early on that I could ask for and receive help when I needed it. I am always reminded by Archangel Michael, "Ask and you shall receive." It only made sense that I could take that assistance one step further and ask for him to help when I was travelling in the dreamtime. I also knew that he couldn't tell me what to do about it until I asked for his help.

I asked him, "Teach me?"

The following technique is what he taught me. I call it "Dreamtime Management."

Putting this into practice on a daily basis totally changed the quality of my sleep. I started to wake up refreshed and energized. The more consistently I did it the calmer I felt during the day. It is my honor to teach you how to do it too.

🌿 Technique 🌿
Dreamtime Management

I have been using this technique for over fourteen years and have taught it to hundreds of my clients and shared it with all of my students. It has been a lifesaver for me and a boost to everyone who uses it regularly. It has even proven to be very easy and effective for young children who are poor sleepers or are very anxious about sleeping.

To help you manage your sleep and get a deep, restful sleep that helps you to wake up fully rested and restored physically and mentally, try this simple exercise. It only takes a minute.

When you get into bed and before you lay down, do the Fear Cord Cutting Technique, page 183, first. Then ask Archangel Michael to help you in the dreamtime. Say out loud or quietly to yourself:

> "Dear Archangel Michael, please be with me as I enter into
> the dreamtime and guide me to the highest levels of spiritual in-
> struction and direction. I ask that while I sleep my entire body

*and aura be surrounded by your healing angels and that I re-
ceive deep, natural healing and rest so that when I wake in the
morning I am fully rested, restored, renewed, and at peace.
Thank you."*

I have learned over the years that we are never alone. Spirit is always with us in one way or another—consciously or subconsciously.
The more I worked with the angels, the more that sense of presence
and guidance developed. I have had many instances in my life when
angels have directly intervened on my behalf and saved my life.

Helping a Loved One

As I started to teach this dreamtime management technique to clients
and students, they began to ask me an interesting question. "If the
lower astral realms is where we can help people, and being in the upper realms is where we can get help for ourselves, what do we do about
helping someone we love?"

A very good question, I thought.

If you are concerned or worried about a particular family member
or friend, you can adjust your request the following way:

*"Dear Archangel Michael, please be with me in the dream-
time and guide me to the highest levels of spiritual instruction
and direction. I also ask for your assistance in helping _____,
with _____. I ask that the answer to this problem be made
crystal clear to me within the next twenty-four hours. I ask that
while I sleep my entire body and aura be surrounded by your
healing angels and that I receive deep, natural healing and rest
so that when I wake in the morning I am fully rested, restored,
renewed, and at peace. Thank you."*

Solving Personal Problems

On the other hand, if you are struggling to find an answer to a personal problem that is causing you concern, try this:

"Dear Archangel Michael, please be with me in the dream-time and guide me to the highest levels of spiritual instruction and direction. I also ask for your assistance in helping me with _____ [describe the situation]. Please make the answer crystal clear to me within the next twenty-four hours on how best to resolve this situation in a loving way for the highest and greatest good of all involved. I ask that while I sleep my entire body and aura be surrounded by your healing angels and that I receive deep, natural healing and rest so that when I wake in the morning I am fully rested, restored, renewed, and at peace. Thank you."

Don't be afraid to be creative in asking for assistance. Whether you believe in angels, God, Allah, Buddha, or are guided by spirits from Mother Nature, they all follow the same spiritual laws of the universe. They cannot and will not interfere with your free will. They can only help when asked, and angels love to be asked. Don't be afraid to ask. *Ever.* They are there to provide assistance and would love to help you. You are not taking them away from anything else. Angels can be everywhere, all the time. There is no request too small or too trivial.

Just remember, when you ask, to be clear about what you need and give them a time frame. Universal time is not the same as man-made time frames. All prayers are answered. If you want an answer sooner, let them know and give them a time frame. I like to request that all answers be received within a specific time period and that the answers be given to me clearly so I can understand them.

If during this exercise you feel like you are making this all up, that is all right. You go right ahead and imagine it anyway. Form always follows thought. If you are uncomfortable working with Angels, but you like to work with Jesus, then by all means go for it. That advice is also true if you prefer to work with God or Mohammed, a specific saint, or an ascended master. It is all the same intent. I do recommend, however, that when you work with the dreamtime management technique you use ascended masters, archangels, Jesus, God, Mohammed, or a

Saint, and not a deceased relative or beloved pet companion. They don't have the same level of universal consciousness to help you effectively ascend and work in the higher spiritual levels of the astral plane.

As you begin to manage your dreamtime, you will begin to notice, in a very short period of time, that there is a dramatic change to your sleep. You will fall asleep faster, wake up more rested, and feel calmer and more alert. I have had clients tell me that it worked immediately and they couldn't believe how much better and more rested they felt after just one day. Others have said it took a few days for them to realize how much more energy they had. Until they started managing their dreamtime, they never realized just how deeply tired they really were. Life felt better, brighter, and easier.

It is also interesting to note that clients reported that when they requested assistance to resolve particular problems in the dreamtime management, solutions always presented themselves within the time frame they requested. The solution was often quite creative and innovative. In some instances, tense relationships suddenly took a turn for the better without anything being said or done. In other situations, issues that couldn't be resolved no longer carried the same level of emotional pain and the person making the dreamtime request was able to move forward with their life in a healthier way.

The most significant result of the dreamtime management were the reports of reduced feelings of stress and anxiety. If you would like to know more about the results from the study I conducted, turn to the Appendix: A 40-Day Practice Using Three Simple Things on page 225 to read comments from volunteers after the completion of the study.

There is nothing quite like a good night's sleep to help you face your day. You wake up feeling happy, restored, and rejuvenated. Being well rested does wonders for helping to reduce stress and anxiety as well as being able to manage your day more effectively. A lot of my clients tell me that they quite enjoy the process when they use the Dreamtime Management technique and are having fun learning how to master this part of their egos and get a great night's sleep.

Being well rested also makes it easier to have more mental and emotional clarity around the thoughts and beliefs that are causing the stress and anxiety in your life. As a result, you begin to notice how the ego has certain well-entrenched attitudes and behaviors that no longer serve your new sense of well-being and contentment. Trying to shift your egos deeply entrenched attitudes out of its comfort zone can be frustrating and make you feel very resistant to change. There is a way, however, and it is through the power of using positive affirmations effectively. I have learned, though, that many of my clients give up within a short period of time of trying to use positive affirmations, and I can understand why. Changing our egos attitudes and beliefs with positive affirmations can be sidetracked by what I call "blips."

7

Shifting Your Thoughts and Assessing Your Beliefs

Positive affirmations can help us to create new beliefs that are powerful, effective, and life changing. But if your ego is beating you up mentally with a constant stream of negative self-talk, it can be hard to switch the channel to something different. Then there is the need for proof. If you are going through all the trouble to change a negative belief, then there should be an instant payout, right?

Not necessarily. And this is where many of us give up.

We expect everything to change immediately and never have a problem again. It doesn't work that way, in my experience. I discovered that changing my mind was the first step, believing the new affirmation was the second step, but the third step, holding true to the new belief as my world started to change, was the tricky part. I started to call them "blips."

What is a blip? In my experience it is the universe's way of helping you to speed up the change to your life by tearing down the old reality and helping you build a new reality. If you don't understand what blips are and how to deal with them, it makes it easy to give up.

We are what we create. Our thoughts become our reality. If you change your reality, there is going to be a change. The ego is resistant to change. This means that it will struggle with any obstacle that is seen as threatening the status quo.

Remember that part of the ego's job is to record beliefs and attitudes without emotional context. When you realize that the old belief is the underlying cause of your stress and anxiety, and you want to change that recording, the ego will resist. It will continuously hit the reset button and replay the old message repeatedly while you try to believe the new one. It is like your ego becomes lazy and just repeatedly hits the reset button. It is the perfect recipe for staying trapped in a stress inducing, anxiety creating, crazy making life.

Where is that reset button!

In actuality, hitting the reset button is the easy part. The hard part is staying the course with the new belief while your old belief changes. Remember there are only two emotions—love and fear. Every thought has to begin somewhere. If our thoughts are created in fear, we are already moving down the wrong road. We become lost.

How do you know for sure if you are lost? When life becomes a struggle and you feel unhappy and anxious all the time. You keep doing the same thing over and over, trapped in the same old patterns. Whether it be at work, with relationships, friends, or your children, everything pretty much feels stuck. You find that your thoughts just go round and round in a pattern of negative self-talk. You begin to believe that finding your way back is a struggle. You fall into a rut. You complain that you have "lost your way" or "don't know which way to turn" or "can't find your purpose."

It is hard to find our way back to love when we are in a constant state of fear. Have you ever asked yourself, "Why does my ego keep me prisoner in this constant state of fear?" For the simple reason, we allow it. We really do seem to struggle with the fact that we have the ability to transform fear into love. When we change our minds, we change our experience. We move from living in fear to living in a state of love. We sometimes lose sight of the fact that changing our life can be that easy.

Remember your ego is just a recorder. It takes what it hears, records it onto a tape in your subconscious mind, and then replays that message back to you whenever you need validation for an experience. It keeps repeating that little gem until something else happens and then it switches to another message if the first one didn't work. On and on it goes until you can't take it anymore. You can try to drown that little voice with booze, sedate it with medication, or even try to tell it to go away and ignore it. But it just keeps on playing in the background like a broken record never giving up. That is until you recognize that you can reprogram the tape.

If you don't like the song, record a new one over it. Your ego will play along—it may argue with you for a while, but it will change. You just have to be persistent with the reprogramming. This is exercising your right to free will.

If, for example, you have been raised to believe that everything you do is wrong, then the ego will replay that belief back to you every single time something happens that turns out to be "wrong" in your opinion. You will treat that replay as proof that you are in fact a failure. This makes you feel powerless, so you stop trying to change anything because you believe that you will only do it wrongly if you try. The repeated experience of failure is the proof that what you have believed from the past is still really true. As a result, you plod along in life feeling unhappy and miserable because you are entrenched in the ego's belief that you can't do anything right.

Have you ever asked yourself, "Is that really true?"

Do you ever question that ego's crazy talk, and ask, "Is your ego always right?" Why do you have to believe it?

Just because something was true as a child doesn't mean it has to be true for you as an adult. When you, as an adult, begin to re-examine what your ego has you believing from past experiences, seize this as an opportunity to see that you have a choice. You can continue to believe the fear that makes you feel powerless or you can create a new belief that empowers you. It is a matter of choice. What would you prefer—a continuous loop that says you are a failure or a continuous loop that reminds you what an amazing human being you really are? I vote for loop number two, thank you very much!

In his book *Journey of Awakening*, Ram Dass relays that "You needn't destroy the ego to escape its tyranny. You can keep this familiar room to use as you wish, and you can be free to come and go. First you need to know that you are infinitely more than the ego room by which you define yourself. Once you know this, you have the power to change the ego from prison to home base" (1990, 6).

Whenever my husband Bert and I are trying to learn a new dance routine, our dance instructor encourages us to keep practicing until it is imprinted into our muscle memory. If you keep dancing in a certain way, your body gets conditioned to doing it automatically without thinking. If we have learned how to do a dance step incorrectly, we have to practice the new steps consciously until it becomes embedded in our subconscious again so we no longer have to think about it. Re-programming your ego's beliefs and providing it with new reference material is the same thing.

If your current dance through life hasn't been working for you, then you are ready for a change. But maybe you aren't sure how to go about it? Well, you can't learn a new dance step if you don't know what is wrong with the old dance step. Look at your current dance with life. What's wrong with it? Are you always finding yourself in love with the wrong person? Is your job becoming a familiar nightmare? Are your friendships always going toxic? What does your ego say to you all the time? What little gems do you hear from your family and friends all the time? What beliefs are making you feel powerless? Write them down.

Once you have unearthed the negative self-talk you can begin to change your dance. The ego is always thinking, always doing. It needs something to work from. If you are going to pull out a negative belief system, then you need to replace it with something positive. The ego doesn't know the difference between positive and negative thoughts, it only knows that it needs to think and retrieve. For every negative belief you uncover, replace it with a positive thought. Think of each positive thought as a new dance step. Learn enough new steps and you have a whole new dance with life that can be exciting, fulfilling, life affirming, and filled with love.

Now, there is one thing that I discovered when I started to work with my ego and reprogram the negative self-talk. Every once in a while a funny thing would happen that would make me pause and wonder if I was doing the right thing. It puzzled me at first, but then I understood.

Each time my husband and I were learning a new dance step we would have to teach our bodies to move in a certain way. In the beginning we would stumble a lot and we would step on each other's toes and have to start over. I found the same thing would happen when I was trying to change an old negative belief into a positive one. I would stumble and need to stop and regroup. I call this little stumble a blip.

What exactly is a blip?

A blip is an energetic bulldozer created by the universe to help you break down the old belief to make room for the new belief. Remember, form always follows thought. If you have a negative belief, it is a well-developed and formulated thought that has created the reality you are currently experiencing. Constructing a new belief system means you are dismantling an old belief system. The universe will help you to do that, if you let it.

For example, say you are someone who has spent their whole life believing they are a failure. Everything you do turns into one failure after another. One day you decide to change your mind. You no longer accept failure and believe that everything you do is a success. But the old failure belief has built a house in your subconscious mind. Your ego visits there every day and recounts all the stories held there. Your new belief wants to build a new house on the same piece of property. The old house has to be torn down to make room for the new house, doesn't it? The universe, which is love, will send in a bulldozer to make it happen faster. The trick is to let the bulldozer do its job so that you can continue moving forward and building your new house.

The first time you experience that bulldozer you will be tempted to run and hide back in your old house, throw up your hands, and say, "All this positive self-talk has been a total waste of time. Look at what is happening to me, I give up."

For most of us, we don't like change. Our ego is quite happy with the status quo, regardless of the consequences. If you try to mess with how your ego runs the show, it will argue with you, fight you, threaten you, or say anything to save itself from learning anything different. It is a lot of bravado, though. Your ego is just frightened. This is why I believe we think change is so hard.

In my private practice I have found it's the blips people encounter when they are trying to turn their life around that makes them stumble and fall back into old patterns.

If you can step aside and keep restating your new belief to the ego and let that bulldozer do its job, you will rebuild your new emotional house a whole lot faster. I know because I have been there, a lot! I have dealt with a few bulldozers in my life and I can tell you from experience that every last blip was totally worth the experience—big time.

Earlier in the book I was relaying how back in the 1980s my husband and I both had jobs working in the hospital lab industry. It was one crazy decade and we were on a merry-go-round that just wouldn't stop spinning. The economy and particularly our health care system in Canada was undergoing a major downturn. As a result, a lot of people lost their jobs or were downsized. You were given a choice: Either accept the new role that came with a very large pay cut or lose your job to another applicant. It was as simple as that. Everybody's wages were frozen. By the time we came out of the '80s, we were financially battered and bruised. We had barely managed to hang onto our house. We had to re-mortgage our home twice just to buy cars so we could keep working. Many of our friends had lost their homes, their businesses, or their jobs completely. It looked like we were going to have to declare bankruptcy. We were terrified of what that meant.

During this time in our life, we often didn't know from week to week if either one of us even had a job. To cope, we started to make a game out of it. Every Monday morning we would call each other and say, "Okay, I'm still working, are you?" Financially we were running on empty. The lowest point for us came when we were out for a walk with our children one day and they wanted to stop for ice cream. Neither one of us had enough money left in our wallets to even buy one ice cream to share between the two of them. We were extremely unhappy, very stressed out, and fearful of what the future held for us.

After we got home from this depressing event, my husband suggested we attend a service at a different church the next day. He said he heard the minister there was going to be giving a talk on abundance.

He said we should hear what she has to say. So, reluctant and annoyed, I went along. I was glad I did.

That sermon proved to be very interesting. Life was never the same for us afterward. The minister talked about negative belief systems and how the universe can only give you what you believe. We had never heard that before and it came as a real shock for us. We just looked at each other with *that* look on our faces. The minister went on to explain that all negative beliefs could be changed once you knew what they were and decided to change them to positive beliefs. I knew we were both thinking the same thing. What did that mean for us? What did we believe that was creating all this financial chaos in our life, and could we really change it?

As soon as we got home we sat down and started to write down all of our beliefs around money. It was an informative exercise and was quite shocking, to be honest. It never occurred to us to examine our beliefs before, especially around money. We just accepted what we had been taught or had learned through experience.

We discovered the following: Bert, as a result of being raised in a very strict protestant faith all of his life, believed that "you couldn't go to heaven if you were rich." I, on the other hand, had been raised on credit cards and really never understood the value of money. If my father had a dollar, he would spend five. I never really handled my own money until I was seventeen because my father took care of everything. Growing up we were always impeccably dressed and ate in the finest of restaurants, but we didn't have much else to speak of. That analysis of my childhood helped me realize that I believed you "had to be poor to be happy" as well as, "better spend it now because it won't be there later." Needless to say, we were both pretty surprised at what our core beliefs revealed about how we were living our lives. It also explained why we always had such interesting discussions around money.

We decided then and there that things were going to change. We made a pact to change to a new belief system. We created an affirmation that best reflected what we wanted in our life, and then we wrote it out. It was: "Our life is filled with joy, happiness, abundance, and prosperity." After repeating this, we then said a special prayer that the minister shared with the congregation. It is from the John Randolph Price book, *The Angels Within Us*. I call it the "Prayer of Abundance."

> *Angel of the Spirit I AM, I invoke your power and force to clear my consciousness of all false beliefs regarding money, and to open wide your Gate and flood my world with the infinite abundance I am and have. I ask this in love and for the good will of all. Let my financial all-sufficiency come forth now for my right use—quickly, easily, and peacefully (1993, 66–67).*

We also promised to help each other through this and support each other when the chips were down. If I was having a bad day and was struggling, my husband would remind me of our new belief, and vice versa. We knew we had some challenges ahead of us, and quite honestly there were days when it was a struggle. The next three months turned out to be quite a ride for our family.

Up to this point in our marriage, if we had managed to save $200, it was a miracle. However, if we did manage to do it, I could guarantee you that within the week something would break down and it would cost $202 to get it fixed. It never failed. It was so predictable that I started to find ways to *not* put any money in our savings account, which drove my husband crazy. Can you see how embedded that belief system was?

Despite our nervousness and uncertainty with affirmations, we started with our new belief system immediately. I wrote out the new belief and prayer and put a copy on each of our bedside tables. We decided that it would be the first thing we would read every morning and again every night before we went to bed. I also wrote out copies and put them on the bathroom mirror and in front of the kitchen sink, and I made one to put on the dashboard of each of our cars so we could read it at stoplights on our way to and from work. Within weeks of that prayer work, it seemed like our lives had changed overnight. We went from being stressed out and nearly bankrupt to having permanent jobs, money in the bank, and a new car. It felt like we could do no wrong. Everything in our lives started to change for the better. Then we experienced our first blip.

After about three months of enjoying all our newfound abundance and accomplishments, we were surprised by a rather auspicious and synchronous event. On this particular day we both happened to arrive home at the same time. That was a first. We worked different shifts in different communities and we had never both come home at the same time before. We walked into the house together laughing and teasing each other about the beauty of synchronicity. The last couple of months had been one marvelous surprise after another. What's not to celebrate and be happy about?

As we entered into the house together, we suddenly heard our two children crying and yelling out to us. They were trapped in the downstairs family room. We immediately ran downstairs, shocked to find our two children standing on the couch surrounded by steaming hot water gushing out from the water heater in the next room. The water heater had literally burst at the seams and was flooding the entire family room with boiling water. By the time we reached the children, there was about an inch of steaming water settling in on the family room floor. My husband ran through the hot water, grabbed each child up under his arms, and carried them over to the stairs. He grabbed some towels, wrapped them around his arms, and managed to turn off water to the heater. After it was all over, the two of us sat on the bottom of the basement stairs and looked in dismay at all the water pooling all over the carpet of the family room. Dazed and confused, we sat there for a while, both speechless. We were devastated.

This was our first blip.

I remember thinking, "How are we supposed to handle this?" It dawned on me that I was so tempted to say, "We are being punished for wanting to get ahead." I felt afraid and thought to myself, "We are not supposed to want to get ahead." That immediately felt all terribly wrong.

That was our fear response.

I turned and looked at my husband and said, "Look, the universe is washing away all our old belief systems." My husband turned and looked at me with disbelief, then he smiled and said, "Yeah, it washed away all of our old beliefs."

That was staying true to our new belief and stepping aside to let the universe bulldoze the old manufactured belief out of the way.

We repeated our new belief and called the company that sold us the water heater. The company was so shocked at what had happened that not only did their firm clean up the basement but they also gave us a brand new water heater, all free of charge. After everything was professionally cleaned and dried out there was absolutely no damage to the basement whatsoever. The carpets, furniture, and drywall— everything was fine and very clean. No mildew or dampness anywhere. That's when we learned how powerful blips could be at clearing away old paradigms.

Our new reality.

A few weeks later we had another blip.

It was a beautiful fall day when I came home after work early to find a city inspector walking around our backyard. A little surprised, I asked if there was a problem. He walked up to me and said, "That chimney on the outside of your house is illegal and has to be removed." I told him we had lived here for over nine years and that it had been installed by the previous owners. I offered to show him the paperwork. He just shrugged his shoulders and said, "You have six weeks to re-move it or face a $25,000 fine for an illegal fireplace installation." With that he handed me his business card and got into his car and drove off. The whole encounter had left me feeling quite shaken and uncertain. We had no idea the previous owners had installed the fireplace with-out a permit.

When my husband arrived home I told him what had happened. He called a family friend, who was a contractor, and he came over right way. He looked at everything and said that depending on the amount of work required we were looking at anywhere from $5,000 to $10,000 to bring everything back up to code. Things were going so well for us, but this was a blow. We were just starting to recover finan-cially and this would set us back quite a bit. Once again we found our-selves at a loss for words. I turned to my husband and said, "It's going to be all right. This is the universe burning away our old belief systems." We repeated our belief and knew that somehow this would all work out. That night my husband decided to go through our purchase agreement, and he found that the previous owners had left us the warranty for the fireplace. He called the company that installed the fireplace. Much to our surprise, we were told that the fireplace was still under warranty.

The company came and made all the necessary repairs covered under the warranty. Everything was brought up to code for a small fee of $500, which we could easily afford. When they were finished replacing the fireplace and packing up to leave, the foreman came and told me that we were lucky we called when we did.

"Oh," I replied, "Why is that?"

He said, "You were days away from having your house burn down."

He went on to explain that the chimney had burned through its liner, and it had started to burn through the insulation. He said it was only a matter of time before the fireplace would have caused the house to burn down. That sent shivers down my spine. We got a new fireplace and the city inspector passed it without incident. Changing our beliefs had once again saved us from a major disaster.

After these two blips, life continued to improve and became more joyful, abundant, and happy. We took our first family vacation in years and had a blast. We have never looked back and are still amazed at how beautifully everything came together back then. We still have the occasional blip around finances, but we just smile and know that our new emotional house is built on a firm foundation of belief that "life is filled with joy, happiness, abundance, and prosperity."

These experiences taught me that when you want to change a negative belief system, the universe gives you an opportunity to clear a lot of old negative energy in a hurry. Blips are the universe asking you "Are you really serious about changing your mind?" This is your moment of truth. It is an opportunity to fast forward. I have since learned from my clients that blips are one of the reasons people give up on trying out new belief systems. They don't understand how blips are there to help them. Instead they see it as a challenge and, out of fear, decide to go back to the old dance. The old way may be harder and challenging, but at least it is familiar and they understand the steps.

🪷 Exercise 🪷
How to Change a Negative Belief System

To change a negative belief system, first pick a negative belief that you want to change. Then decide on what you want your new belief to be. Keep the new belief statement in the current tense and upbeat. For example, instead of "I want more abundance," you would write, "I am abundance," or "My life is filled with abundance." You could make it even more powerful by saying, "My life is filled with abundance every day, in every way."

Write out the new belief system on several small recipe cards. Place the cards in prominent places around the house where they will be seen all the time: the bathroom mirror, dressing room mirror, sink, above the stove, on the fridge, on the dashboard of your car, and beside the bed. Put a copy in your wallet to review when you are waiting for an appointment.

The new belief system is the first thing you say to yourself every morning and the last thing you say to yourself every night. Repeat the new belief every time you look at it. If you are waiting in traffic, say the new belief to yourself. Repeat the belief to yourself whenever you are having any negative thoughts. Keep this up for forty days. Repeating your new belief for forty days is necessary because that's how long it takes for your ego and subconscious mind to reprogram its habitual responses to how it responds to life's challenges. After the forty days, you can choose to deal with another negative belief system or you can continue to use the original one.

How to Handle Blips

If you can stay steadfast and true to your new belief system, then any blip will get rid of a lot of negative energy in your life very quickly. It helps to remember that blips are only the universe's way of helping you onto the fast track of enjoying the benefits of the new belief, by clearing a lot of garbage out of the way in the shortest period of time.

It will help to clear out the old emotional house and give you an opportunity to build a new one. I believe that God is only love and he wants us to succeed, but our egos are very good at being afraid of that success.

Blips can be a little intimidating at first. Remember the power of choice. The universe isn't going to send you anything you can't handle. Dance the new dance even while you are stumbling with the new steps. If at any time you are dealing with the preconceived negative issue, just keep saying your new belief to yourself. You will find that the issue will just peter out and what you thought would be a big problem is just a minor misunderstanding.

Life does not happen to you—you create the experience

If you change what you believe, you change your experience. Don't be afraid of the change. It is as simple as that.

When we change our core negative belief systems, we are literally rebuilding our emotional foundation. It takes time to tear down the old emotional house, hence the forty days. It also takes time to build a new emotional house. Be patient with yourself. Don't run away from the blips. View them with optimism and confidence. Stand firm and reaffirm your new belief. It's only the universe working to help you. It's also helpful to remember that after the forty days, changes can still be happening up to a year later, even if you have moved onto changing another old belief system.

For my husband and I, some things happened very quickly and others took some time. What mattered was that within a year our life experience was totally different and we have never looked back.

Once you get the knack of changing old beliefs and learning how to reprogram the inner ego, you may be surprised at how quickly some of the changes can happen. Don't be afraid to make a game out of it. Dance with your ego. Give it a new experience. Embrace the crazy mind-talk and teach your ego something new.

Part III
Protecting
Your Energy

As you begin to work with your intuition, you might begin to notice an interesting sensation. You start to notice how much you can actually feel going on around you. In the beginning you might find this curious and intriguing. But sooner or later that curiosity will shift to pondering the thought: "If I can feel them, then they can feel me." This might lead you to wonder about your own privacy. It could make you feel a little vulnerable and uncertain.

Beyond the ethics of how and when to use your intuitive abilities, there are several energy techniques to help you not only create your own privacy, but also how to protect it and know when your emotional boundaries are being challenged.

There are several different techniques to help you create your own energetic privacy: shielding, cloaking, and the White Light of Protection. Each technique provides its own level of privacy and protection. Shielding, for example, is very effective to use in the workplace, whereas cloaking would be appropriate when you want complete privacy out in public. Learning how to protect yourself energetically with white light is the big gun—used when you feel the need to be totally safe in unhealthy situations.

Learning how to maintain your emotional boundaries is also most important. There is an art to learning when others are trying to manipulate you by attacking your ego's vulnerabilities. I call them energy tyrants. An energy tyrant is similar to an energy vampire, but instead of sucking you dry, they try to impose their will and control your thoughts and actions. A subset of the energy tyrant is the emotional blackmailer. This form of bullying is the most insidious of all the types of energy tyrants. Often misunderstood and overlooked, you will discover how to recognize energy tyrants and deal with them while maintaining your self-respect and dignity.

8

Creating Shields

I find actively engaging my intuition to be a very liberating experience. Life feels more alive, intricate and interactive. Every experience offers different perspectives and becomes rich with feelings. I was pleasantly surprised at how much I could actually feel. There were times, however, when I started to wonder if perhaps I was feeling too much, all the time. I wanted to be able to turn it down a notch or two. I wondered if there was a way to manage it somehow and have some complete energetic privacy when I choose to have it.

Fortunately, there are three ways to manage how much you feel and when. All the techniques are simple and easy to use. Each can be given its own one word to access at a moment's notice. The first technique is called Shields Up. This technique allows you to safely be aware of what you are feeling and not be drained by other people's emotions. The next technique is called Cloaking, and it provides complete privacy when you need it. The third technique is the White Light of Protection, which is the ultimate energetic protection. It is most appropriately used in situations that may become volatile and unpredictable.

All three techniques help you to maintain crystal clear boundaries about what belongs to you energetically and emotionally. Each technique is flexible and adaptable, depending on the situation you find yourself in. All three types of protection will hold in a crisis.

How I Evolved the Shields Up Technique

When I was newly married, my husband and I moved 5,000 miles away to another part of the country. It was the first time in my life that I was totally on my own. Bert travelled all the time. He left on Mondays and didn't return until Friday night. I was a very young bride in a strange town on the other side of the country with no friends. Thankfully, it didn't take long for me to find a job in my field as a laboratory technologist at a local lab. However, I soon discovered that for all my self-confidence and bravado I was becoming nervous about everything, very quickly. I really tried to fit in at work, but I was just plain different from the other girls. I settled into a familiar routine of holding myself emotionally safe by going to work, coming home, reading, and being by myself. It was the safest thing to do and it was where I felt the most comfortable. I became withdrawn and didn't really feel alive until my husband came home on the weekends. He tried to help but he was trying to establish his career. He couldn't understand why the independent woman he had married suddenly became so emotionally needy and afraid all the time.

In our second year of marriage funny things started happening to me. I would go into work and start to feel these waves of emotion. Some days it was almost unbearable. It seemed to shift depending on who I was sitting next to at the lab bench. I didn't understand it and thought it was something that I was doing. My work started to suffer and my manager was rechecking my work at the end of day. That really upset me. I couldn't stay focused and I wanted to cry all the time. One day it all came to a head. Someone said something to me and I started to cry and couldn't stop. My husband was called and asked to pick me up. I was told to take a week off and get some rest. I slept for days. One afternoon I woke up to find a spirit standing in my bedroom. I had never seen a spirit this clearly or with that much detail. It really rattled me.

I called my mother and told her what had been happening to me and she said that I was obviously beginning to develop the ability to feel other people's energy fields. "It was only a matter of time before that intuitive ability of yours opened up again," she said. "Now it is time to learn how to manage it when you are out in the world," she went on to say. You know there are some things in life that you wish people would tell you in advance. This was definitely one of THOSE moments!

A few days later my mother, who was an artist traveling around the country in a camper van, pulled into our driveway completely unannounced. I was unbelievably relieved to see her. She said it was time to learn how to handle what I was going through. My mother explained to me that over the years she had learned some tricks from her Theosophy teacher on how to deal with this ability to feel other people's energy. My very skeptical husband was duly shooed away and my mother set up a meditation circle in the middle of our living room. She lit some candles and some incense, and then we sat down and went into a meditation together.

My mother proceeded to take me through a technique called the White Light of Protection, which pulls down the white light of divine love from the heavens and surrounds your aura and protects it from all outside influences. She explained to me that learning how to use this would help me cope and help to shield me from other people's negative thoughts and opinions. It only took a minute to learn how to do it. It was a cool little technique, I thought. My mother explained the importance of practicing it every day to enhance its protection. She also told me that if I practiced it daily, it would help to increase my spiritual vibration. This in turn would help me on my path of spiritual awareness.

After we were done I asked my mother why this was happening to me now. She explained that with the advent of the '60s, the planet began to shift in group consciousness. It was the dawning of the Age of Aquarius: The Love Revolution. It was a time of free love, peace, marches, and anti-war demonstrations that the world had never seen before. Young people around the world were rising up and asking why. As a result of this shift in global consciousness, an interesting thing began to happen to our planet energetically. The veil between heaven and earth began to thin. People were reporting that they could feel and sense things they had never felt before. Suddenly being psychic was being "in." This shift explained why I too, was starting to see spirits more clearly, and not just as shadows or impressions as I had in the past.

The White Light of Protection technique has been around in one form or another for several centuries. It has been used by spiritualists, shamans, alchemists, and spiritual healers as a way to protect themselves from being influenced or harmed by any negative energies from other people, places, or situations. The technique came back into vogue during the 1960s when the shift in world consciousness picked up momentum. People were feeling the increased need to protect themselves energetically as they started to reconnect to their natural inborn abilities of being intuitive.

The White Light of Protection behaves like a shield, and it protects you from another person's energy. This energy can also be tasked to stop other people from attacking you, feeling you, or attaching to your energy field or aura. It also means that if someone is feeling angry, upset, or anxious, that person's energy can't enter your energy field and affect you because the white light simply makes it slide off your aura.

Despite the fact that it was so quick and easy to learn, I quickly ran into a little snag. It didn't work for me all the time. When I mentioned this to my mother, she told me I just needed to practice it more, and so I did. After making more of an effort to practice it daily, I noticed it still sort of worked but not always effectively. I did find it easier to cope with being around other people, but there were some days it didn't matter how hard I tried, I could still feel everything and get overwhelmed. After a couple of years I just gave up and forgot about it—for about twenty years to be exact—until one day when I was at the hairdressers, of all places. The woman sitting next to me started to tell me about this class she was going to take that evening. She said, "It is this really cool technique called the White Light of Protection." Intrigued, I asked her for the teacher's phone number and called to see if there were any more spots left that evening. I thought maybe I needed to relearn how to do it and then maybe it would work for me.

Well, didn't that class just turn out to be a little eye-opener! The instructor taught us a variation of the White Light technique that changed how it worked for me. She taught us how to bring the white light INTO our body and then channel it into our hearts. Once our hearts were full, we then opened up our heart chakras and allowed the white light to pour OUT into our energy field and visualize it surrounding us like a great big eggshell.

For the first time ever, using the white light of protection really worked for me. I was *thrilled*! I was just running around doing my little white light thing all over the place. I was one happy little camper. By this stage of my life I was working as a corporate manager, and that variation of the technique was a major lifesaver for me. My job required that I attend a lot of meetings. Using that variation of the technique on a daily basis had me walking out of those meetings feeling great, instead of feeling like I had just been beaten up with a baseball bat.

Then my life changed dramatically.

I collapsed at work one day. A few days later, as I recovered at home, I had a near-death experience that changed my whole life from top to bottom. I had some pretty miraculous things happen over the next few months that resulted in a total 180-degree change in my life. I had a miraculous recovery despite being told by medical specialists that it would be at least two years before I would be strong enough to return to work. I was back at work in three months.[3] The day I returned to work, though, I knew my life had changed. I didn't belong in the corporate world anymore. A short time later I tendered my resignation and left a very secure corporate position that I loved to train as a healer. It was a leap of faith that I have never regretted. Within a year I was running a very busy private practice out of my home.

As I was training in the healing arts, I was told that it was important to learn how to manage my energy so that I didn't feel drained at the end of the day. No problem I thought, I know how to do the White Light of Protection. After a while though, I started to notice that my clients seemed to respond to me differently than they did to my teacher. My

---

3. My story is detailed in my first book, *Following Body Wisdom: How Energy Medicine Can Help Heal.*

teacher got hugged all the time. My clients would ask to shake my hand. Hmmm? I asked myself, "What was I missing?"

One day I happened to be downtown having a coffee with a colleague when a client of mine sat down in the next booth. She didn't see me and I didn't say hi. We respect our clients need for privacy, so I always wait for clients to acknowledge me first, just in case. A short time later a friend joined her in the booth. I overheard her friend ask my client, "How was your session with that lady, Atherton?"

"Oh, it was lovely," she said. "I really enjoyed it and I couldn't believe how much better I felt, but you know, she is a really nice lady but you just can't feel her. You feel like you are being held at arms-length and that it's not okay to get close."

I was stunned. I looked at my colleague who had also overheard the same conversation. She just smiled and shrugged her shoulders. I asked my friend, "What am I doing wrong?"

She said, "I don't know what you are doing, but it is really hard to feel close to you. What have you been doing to protect yourself?"

That's when it dawned on me. The White Light of Protection was just that—protection—and protection meant being impregnable. I didn't need protection from my clients. It was my job to stay centered from a place of love and compassion, but I didn't need to protect myself from attack. I needed to shield my energy so that I could still sense and feel them but not get attached to their field. My clients needed to feel me and not get attached to me either. Using the White Light of Protection put me in a fear stance not a love stance. That was not what healing work was about. It was also not how I wanted to live my life. I wanted to come from a place of inner calm—a place of love—not ego-based fear.

I needed to come up with an alternative that would be more flexible and loving. Remember: being in the dance between the ego and the inner calm means being comfortable feeling what other people are feeling and not reacting to it. I needed to find a way to do that and continue to come from a place of love.

I went back to the preverbal drawing board to figure out what needed to change with the White light of Protection technique I was using.

As I went into meditation, I set the intent to learn and understand how to shield myself while holding space in love and compassion. I quickly found myself having a vision where I was being led to a stone platform by Archangel Gabriel. I was invited to step up onto the platform. When I was standing in the middle of the platform, a violet light came up from the base of the stone and started to fill my energy field and body with violet light. The light washed through me and all around me. It washed through every cell in my body. My breathing became more relaxed, deeper. I felt at peace. Then the light changed to a soft shade of pink and again washed around me and through me. I felt loved, cherished, and safe. Then the light changed to indigo blue and I felt connected and energetic and concepts felt clearer. Then the light turned into a clear shade of green. I felt healing energy. My muscles relaxed and my head felt clearer. I understood that I was being shown how each color passing through my field meant different things and created different results.

It was explained to me by Archangel Gabriel that when I connected to universal energy I could ask for and receive different vibrations represented by the different colors. He helped me to understand that when I connected to the universal energy of pink, people could feel me, touch me, and feel love, but they couldn't attach or come into my field. I could be aware of my own feelings and their feelings at the same time and not be affected by what they were feeling. In this way, it was explained that I could be fully connected and present in a state of love and grace. People wouldn't feel disconnected from me; they would feel love.

Going through this exercise with the angels showed me what wasn't working for me when I was using the White Light of Protection technique. I recognized that it was an excellent form of divine protection from any and all outside elements, but it does cut you off from being connected to others. Sometimes very necessary—but not required all the time.

Learning when to use the White Light of Protection and when to use shielding was the next step. There is a time and a place for all things.

How you decide to protect yourself energetically is no different. Luckily there are options that are simple, safe, flexible, and adaptable.

🪷 Technique 🪷
The Shields Up

The purpose of using the Shields Up technique is to help you be present in a loving, compassionate way that feels safe and steady while you are around other people. It will help you to be clear about what is yours and what belongs to the other person. You can still sense and feel them. They will still be able to sense and feel you. The difference will be that you cannot pick up their energy and carry it and they cannot attach to you.

Shields Up!
Make yourself comfortable and begin to take slow, easy breaths.

Go into your Vertical Axis using the full technique or your one word. (The Vertical Axis Technique, Step-by-Step, page 93)

> *Feeling present in the energy of the Vertical Axis, bring your attention to your heart center. Feel yourself centered and grounded into heaven and earth. Breathe slowly and steadily.*
>
> *Now ask the energy of the Vertical Axis to fill your heart with the soft pink energy of Divine Love.*
>
> *Sense or feel the energy of the Vertical Axis turning into a soft shade of pink. Feel it filling up your heart. As your heart fills up, it begins to open and expand outward. The energy of the soft pink light of Divine Love begins to move out from your heart and into your body.*
>
> *Feel the energy of Divine Love moving out of your heart and into your chest and down into your arms, moving up into your shoulders, neck, and head. Feel it moving down into your abdomen, your legs, your feet, and your toes.*
>
> *Feel the energy of Divine Love filling up your body, filling every cell and every organ with the pink energy of Divine Love.*

Now begin to see, sense, or imagine that your entire body is filled to capacity with the soft pink light of Divine Love.

Now see the energy of Divine Love in your heart expanding and flowing out of your heart and filling your entire aura. See the light swirling down around your feet and wrapping around you. Feel the energy wrapping about your toes and around your legs, hips, abdomen, chest, neck, and both of your arms. Feel it wrapping around your neck and head and moving out into to the very edge of your aura.

Feel the energy of Divine Love inside your body, filling every organ and cell.

See your entire aura filled and surrounded by the soft pink light of Divine Love.

Now pause here for a moment. Feel the energy of this soft pink energy of Divine Love. See, sense, feel, or imagine this energy inside you and surrounding you like an eggshell.

Now set the intent for the pink energy of Divine Love.

State or affirm: "With this energy of Divine Love, people can feel me and touch me but cannot attach, connect, or come into my field. When they feel me, they feel love and compassion. When I feel others, I remain calm and present from a place of compassion, empathy, and grace."

Now open your eyes and take a deep breath, knowing that the energy is with you for the rest of the day. You need not worry about it or think about it, just know it to be true.

I found that being in the Vertical Axis and combining it with the Shields Up did a lovely job of helping me to stay clear about what was mine and what belonged to someone else. Over time I also noticed it helped to reduce stress and anxiety because I wasn't reacting so much to other people's energy. It taught me that how others choose to live and react in the world was not my responsibility, nor was it my task to correct. They had free will just as much as I did. I found myself becoming free from other people's dramas or fears.

Personally, I use the Shields Up technique with soft pink light all the time. It helps me to stay present, aware, and allows me to stand from a place of love and compassion. It has become a loving way to protect my energy when I am working with clients. The added bonus is that I don't feel exhausted at the end of the day. I also get hugged all the time now. I love it!

Create Shields Up with One Word

If you would like to have one word to take you into the Shields Up technique at a moment's notice, then try this procedure:

Make yourself comfortable and begin to take slow, easy breaths.

Go into your Vertical Axis using the full technique or your one word. (The Vertical Axis Technique, Step-by-Step, page 93)

Go into the Shields Up technique. (Shields up! Page 140)

After you set your intent, ask the energy of Vertical Axis to gift you one word that will take you into your shield at a moment's notice. Now open your eyes and take a deep breath, knowing that the energy is with you for the rest of the day. You need not worry about it or think about it, just know it to be true.

The White Light of Protection

The White Light of Protection is an extremely effective technique to use any time you find yourself in a situation that makes you feel threatened. It is also useful any time you want to feel safe and protected.

A few years ago I was in England on a training course. My husband was flying in after my course was over and we had arranged to meet up in London at Victoria Station. I wasn't used to travelling alone and felt a little scared. Before I left for the train station, I felt it was a good idea to use the White Light of Protection, as it had always helped me in the past to feel calmer and reassured that I was being divinely guided and protected. When I arrived at Victoria Station, I quickly became lost. As I wandered around trying to figure out where to go, I suddenly felt a shift in my energy field. It pulled in tight and I felt danger. I heard my intuitive voice say, "Look around." I quickly moved over to a wall and stood with my back to it. As I stood there in Victoria Station with hundreds of people rushing about, I scanned the crowd. There in the distance was a young man looking at me. I knew instantly that I had been targeted by a thief. I looked at him and he looked at me. He stepped back when I made eye contact. You could tell it rattled him. He became a little dazed and confused and quickly faded into a crowd of tourists moving around him. I knew the White Light of Protection had saved me from harm. With a sigh of relief I got my bearings and saw where I needed to go. The remainder of my trip through England was pleasant and safe.

🪷 Technique 🪷
White Light of Protection

To perform the White Light of Protection technique, make yourself comfortable and begin to take slow, easy breaths.

Go into your Vertical Axis using the full technique or your one word. (The Vertical Axis Technique, Step-by-Step, page 93)

Feeling present in the energy of the Vertical Axis, bring your attention to your heart center. Feel yourself centered and grounded into heaven and earth. Breathe slowly and steadily.

Now ask the energy of the Vertical Axis to fill your heart with the White Light of Protection.

Sense or feel the energy of the Vertical Axis turning into a clear white light. Feel it filling up your heart. As your heart fills up, it begins to open and expand outward. The energy of the white light begins to move out from your heart and into your body.

Feel the energy of white light moving out of your heart and into your chest and down into your arms, moving up into your shoulders, neck, and head. Feel it moving down into your abdomen, your legs, your feet, and your toes.

Feel the energy of white light filling up your body, filling every cell and every organ with the energy of white light.

Now begin to see, sense, or imagine that your entire body is filled to capacity with the energy of the white light.

Now see the energy of white light in your heart expanding and flowing out of your heart and filling your entire aura. See the light swirling down around your feet and wrapping around you. Feel the energy wrapping about your toes and around your legs, hips, abdomen, chest, neck, and both of your arms. Feel it wrapping around your neck and head and moving out into to the very edge of your aura.

Feel the energy of the white light inside your body, filling every organ and cell.

See your entire aura filled and surrounded by the white light.

Now pause here for a moment. Feel the energy of the White Light of Protection. See, sense, feel, or imagine this energy inside you and surrounding you like an eggshell.

State or affirm: "The White Light of Protection now blocks all negative energy and ungrounded energy from entering my field. I am divinely guided and protected from all harm. No one can attach, connect, or enter my field in any way. They can see me, feel me, and touch me, but they cannot harm me in any way physically, mentally, emotionally, or spiritually. Only love and positive feelings can enter." Amen.

Now open your eyes and take a deep breath, knowing that the energy of the White Light of Protection is with you for the rest of the day. You need not worry about it or think about it, just know it to be true.

🪷 Exercise 🪷
The White Light of Protection Using One Word

If you would like to have one word to take you into the White Light of Protection at a moment's notice, then try this procedure:

Make yourself comfortable and begin to take slow, easy breaths.

Go into your Vertical Axis. (The Vertical Axis technique, Step-by-Step, page 93)

Call in the White Light of Protection. (White Light of Protection technique, page 143)

After you have set your intent, ask the energy of the Vertical Axis to gift you one word that will take you into the White Light of Protection at a moment's notice.

Now open your eyes and take a deep breath, knowing that the energy of the White Light of Protection is with you for as long as you need it on this day. You need not worry about it or think about it, just know it to be true.

Energetic Privacy

Maintaining your emotional boundaries also means being able to exercise your right to create energetic privacy and vice versa. It is perfectly normal to need or expect time to be left alone to ponder, heal, or reflect in order to put the perspective and sanity back into your life. A line that has always been attributed to actress Greta Garbo says it so beautifully: I want to be alone. There is nothing wrong with that.

Women in particular always seem to feel guilty when they feel this desperate need to be left alone from time to time. In our society there seems to be this consistent subtle message that to be successful, women need to be superhuman. So we put on our capes and fly out into the world and work very hard to be it *all*, all the time—wife, mother, supervisor, employee, household manager, nurse, cook, maid, lover, activity coordinator, and best friend. Superwoman. Men, as well, suffer from expectations of having to be all things, all the time—husband, father, provider, champion, protector, guardian, leader, caretaker, gardener, handyman, and mechanic. I call it the white knight syndrome. For both men and women, any need to be left alone from time to time can be viewed as a threat to the relationship; both men and women suffer from an inability to step out of their superhuman role and respect their emotional and energetic needs.

Emotional and energetic boundaries can be weakened and challenged by any type of unreal or fearful emotional expectation. Whether

these expectations are of your own making or as a result of work, relationships, or responsibilities, these challenges only serve to create more
fear and increase our anxiety and stress levels.

Feelings create energy that radiates out from the aura. This energy
can be shared, whether we are consciously aware of it or not. Once
again we look to the human body as being like musical tuning forks.
Tap one and the other begins to vibrate too. Our auras respond the
same way. We can pick up on the vibrations from the people around
us. Some feel it more than others. Our emotions can be triggered energetically by what we watch on TV, hear on the radio, or see in public.
We can pick up and react to the emotional energy from a phone conversation or something we have read in the paper or online. If our
child is hurt, we feel their pain. If our lover is unhappy, we empathize
with their unhappiness and try to help them be happy again. If our
friend is in crisis, we worry for them and try to help them find a solution. Trying to be the superhero and deal with all of these additional
demands take their toll on our emotional boundaries. It adds additional stress to an already stressful life.

If your emotional boundaries are subjected to enough long-term
stress or anxiety like this, your physical body and energy body can become worn out and depleted. Sooner or later something will give out.
Emotionally, you can begin to feel vulnerable, unsure, foggy, angry, or
irritable, just to name a few. Physically, you can feel run down, achy,
dizzy, nauseated, and you can have headaches or consistent digestive
upsets; sleep patterns can become irregular. Some of my clients reported feeling physically and emotionally defenseless, weak, disempowered, useless, and frightened. They had difficulty processing any
information clearly, and they would stutter or feel short of breath. The
list is endless.

When this happens, it is called "being left wide open." It means that
you are picking up so much information energetically that your body
and mind can no longer differentiate between what is yours and what
belongs to someone else. It can make you feel like you are short-circuiting and in total sensory overload.

When this happens to my clients, they report that they feel like they would give anything to be able to run and hide from the world. They crave or pray for even a few precious moments of peace and quiet. Every thought, feeling, or gesture feels down right painful. Some report that it felt like they were hit with a bolt of lightning that seared through their muscles. It came on so quickly that they froze emotionally and couldn't respond or act. The effect of being wide open often resulted in panic attacks and extreme anxiety. When you are this wide open, it is virtually impossible to clearly understand your intuition.

Years ago, I collapsed at work from stress overload. It felt like my knees were knocking and I was dizzy and disorientated. I passed out. When I came to, my heart was racing and the ambulance crew thought I was having a heart attack. I spent days curled up in bed, exhausted and overwhelmed. Talking to anyone was agonizing. Anyone who has experienced feeling wide open like this will agree that it can be a scary place to be in and a hard one to bounce back from.

When we are in this emotionally and physically vulnerable place, the ego mind steps up and acts as our protector and guardian. It earnestly tries to find a way to fix the overload, and the ego goes into defense mode. Anything or everything can become very confusing. It has a heyday and creates all these mind arguments that, in the grand scheme of things, don't make any sense. Did Mary really say that? Did John really mean what he said? Do my kids hate me? Am I a bad mother? Why is my boss avoiding me? Did I do something wrong? Does my husband really love me? Why are my friends avoiding me? My mother never loved me? Why hasn't Jane returned my phone call? The list goes on and on.

As your mind swirls around in chaos with senseless mind arguments or perceived fears, you start to lose perspective. It is almost impossible to decipher between what is real and what is unreal, imagined, or feared. The line between fear and truth become blurred. This is when your emotional boundaries are the most battered and bruised. That's when you find yourself desperately trying to find any way to get off the merry-go-round. You just want and need everyone to shut up and go away. You want to go back and be present with the peace and love of the inner calm.

Finding time to get away and be alone so that you can tap into the inner calm and get your bearings straight isn't always possible when you have responsibilities. In these situations, it is helpful to know that there is a way to protect your field so you can have some energetic privacy until you can be alone. It is called cloaking.

The Cloak of Privacy

The Cloak of Privacy is a gentle, easy way to surround yourself with an additional layer of protection. The cloak lets you dial back and disconnect from all the outside influences. You can hear your intuitive guidance more easily and get your perspective back. Imagine, if you will, being like Harry Potter with his invisibility cloak, only this doesn't make you invisible, it just makes you impervious to other people's energy.

Creating the Cloak of Privacy is easy and simple to do. You can wear it all the time or put it on when you feel you need it. It is yours and yours alone. It is a gift to you from the universe. Its sole purpose is to give you privacy when you are in public, in a loving way.

❧ Technique ❧
The Cloak of Privacy

To discover your cloak of privacy you will need a journal and a pen. You will want some colored pencils or crayons so you can draw what your cloak looks like. It is important that you will not be disturbed. This exercise will take about thirty minutes.

Make yourself comfortable and take a few moments to feel relaxed and calm. Take a few deep breaths and close your eyes. Go into your Vertical Axis. (The Vertical Axis technique, Step-by-Step, page 93)

Now imagine or pretend that you are standing in a well-lit room with no windows and one door at the end of the room. Walk over to the door and open it. When you open the door, imagine that you are looking into another very large room filled with sunlight. As you look around, you can see that the room is surrounded on three sides with very large windows that are all open to the outdoors.

As you look through the windows you can see a beautiful meadow with soft grass, trees, and flowers of every color growing everywhere you look. You can feel a soft, warm breeze blowing in from the windows. The air is scented with the aroma of the flowers. You can see and hear the birds singing as they fly through the air.

In the middle of the room you notice there is a beautiful, large wooden table. The sides and legs of the table are carved with the images of angels and animals of all shapes and sizes. In the middle of the table there is a large box. Now see yourself walking over to the table and drawing the box toward you.

Take a moment to examine the box. Run your hands over the box. What is the box made of? Is it cardboard or wood? Is it flat or does it have a shape to it? Are there any images on the box? If there are, what are they? Write down what you see, feel, and sense.

Now open the box and look inside. Imagine or pretend that you can see your cloak of privacy inside the box. Lift it out and lay it out on the table. What does the cloak look like? Is it long or short? Does it have a hood? What is the cloak made of? Is the cloak made of fabric or animal skin? If it is an animal skin, know that this animal has gifted you its protection and guidance. It is an honor to the animal if you will accept it. Take a moment to thank the spirit of the animal and its gift to you. If the cloak is made of fabric, what kind of fabric is it? Is it cotton, silk, velvet, or some other material you are familiar with? What color is your cloak? How is your cloak decorated? If so, what is it decorated with? Stones, beads, gems, thread, symbols? Take a moment to draw out what you see and feel or sense.

Now open your cloak up and look inside the cloak. What kind of fabric is inside the cloak? What color is it? Are there any symbols inside? Pick it up. Try it on. How does it feel?

Take a moment to write down your thoughts and feelings about your cloak.

Now, continuing to breathe deeply, slowly open your eyes and feel yourself becoming aware of your space. Look around the room and move your fingers and toes. Get up and walk around.

Feel yourself being fully present and aware of your surroundings.

This is your cloak of privacy. It is your cloak and yours alone. There is no other cloak like it. This cloak is a gift to you from the universe. It will keep you safe and give you privacy whenever you ask for it. When you wear your cloak, people will not be able to read you. It will hold you safe and protect you when you are feeling vulnerable and overwhelmed.

You can choose when to put your cloak on or when to take it off. It is your decision. When you are not wearing it, it can be placed back here in the box, or you can create a special closet for it in this room. This room is yours alone. No one can enter this room but you.

When you are ready, take off your cloak and hang it up in your sacred room or put it back into the box. If you feel like you are making this all up, that's all right. Go ahead. Remember, form always follows thought.

Take a few minutes to journal what your experience was like. Look at the drawing you made of your cloak. How does your cloak make you feel? Take your time. Review your thoughts and feelings. Be gentle with yourself. If you feel you cannot draw your cloak, write out a description. If you feel like you are making it all up—go ahead, make it up, and have some fun with it. The universe is guiding your imagination.

How to Use Your Cloak of Privacy

Learning how and when to use your cloak can be fun. There are three simple ways you can access your cloak. One way is to imagine going into your sacred room to retrieve your cloak. All you have to do is think about your sacred room, go to the box, open it, and put on the cloak. It only takes a moment. Or you can imagine or pretend to put it on using a thought, such as "cloak on" or "cloak off." A third way is to ask the universe for one word that will put your cloak of privacy on or off at a moment's notice. Whenever you are not wearing your cloak, imagine or pretend that it is in your special box or closet.

Any of these steps should only take a moment. If it takes more than fifteen seconds to put your cloak on, then you are putting too much effort into it. The universe likes things to be simple and easy. The ego likes to make things complicated and difficult. I find that to be a good reminder.

Personally, I use my cloak of privacy all the time when I am out in public, especially if I am going to be in large groups, such as at a mall, movie theater, lecture, or grocery store. For me, the cloak of privacy is a reminder that I don't have to "read" or "see" people energetically when I am out in the world. It also gives me permission to be clear about my emotional boundaries so that I am not overwhelmed by what is happening around me. It doesn't interfere with my intuition, but it does give me energetic privacy from reacting to everything that my aura comes into contact with when I am out in public.

The only time I will fully uncloak is when I am in the treatment room with a client and I need to see and feel their energy so that I can be of assistance on their healing journey. I have no interest in reading the grocery clerk or the salesperson. I respect my privacy and I respect theirs. Although, clients tell me that when they see me walking downtown it always looks like I am floating from store to store. I smile in acknowledgement knowing that they are sensing and feeling my cloak from a distance.

Practice using your cloak when you are in public. See what happens when you are fully cloaked. What happens when you are not cloaked? Does it feel different? Have some fun with it. See if people look at you differently or if they look right through you. Do you find people bumping into you when you wear it? Try wearing it in the department store and see if clerks offer you any assistance. Then take it off and see what happens. It is an interesting experience.

I have also found cloaking to be very helpful when dealing with people who have poor emotional boundaries. These are the people that leave you feeling totally depleted. It can be confusing and frustrating, and they can leave you feeling concerned that you caused it somehow. That is never the case.

9

Recognizing Energy Tyrants

Have you ever gone to a party and felt like you had the life sucked right out of you? Have you ever had a conversation with someone and felt totally drained afterward? Do you ever get a gut ache before you call a certain relative? Do you feel like you have to brace yourself before you can help a certain friend? What about the colleague at work who lives from one breathless crisis to another? If you have answered yes to any of these questions, then you have encountered an energy tyrant.

In the very early days of my practice I was really pumped up to "be of service." I felt like there was nothing I couldn't do to help someone. My ego started to get the best of me. I was invited to a party that was being held by a colleague of mine. When I arrived at the party, there was a man on the other side of the room. He took one look at me and made a beeline across the room to talk to me. He had heard of me but we had never met before. It was hard not to be flattered by the attention, of course. He wanted to know about *everything* I did. Naturally, I was more than eager to share the possibilities of what energy work had to offer. He started to pepper me with questions regarding his litany of health concerns. Yet every time I tried to answer him he would instantly interrupt me. I couldn't get a word in edgewise. I remember feeling frustrated and thinking to myself, "How on earth does this man even get out of bed in the morning if he is this sick?"

People standing around us started to move away. I suddenly found myself standing in a corner alone with him. I started to feel woozy and nauseated. Each time I stepped back, he would step forward. Eventually I found myself trapped with my back up against a wall. He wouldn't stop talking! I felt confused and disorientated. The poor man was desperate to be heard. I tried to empathize but I felt utterly trapped. Finally, in sheer desperation, I feigned a headache and quickly retreated to the bathroom to recuperate. I was frightened and felt vulnerable. I was angry with myself for getting ensnared in a conversation like that. I was angry that I felt sorry for him. Then I felt guilty because I couldn't handle the situation. I felt foolish and naïve—an amateur. I had let myself become defenseless. I made my excuses to the hostess and went home early. I was too upset to stay and be sociable anymore.

When I arrived home, I sat down and had a good cry. A few days later, still feeling disturbed and upset about what happened at the party, I called one of my teachers and told her what had happened. She told me I had been cornered by an "energy tyrant." That was a shock. It explained everything though. I was oblivious to what was happening at the time. He had poor emotional boundaries and I didn't know, at the time, how to hold mine.

As I sat in mediation to mull over what had happened and what to do about it, I was reminded that there is no excuse for bad behavior. We all want to help others, and then there are times when we need to help ourselves. I started to ask myself where to draw the line. When does someone cross the line? Is it all right to draw the line? I needed to know how to be clear about my emotional boundaries.

Emotional Boundaries

As you become more aligned with your intuitive abilities, you may be struggling with what your ego thinks they are. Boundaries could be perceived as coming across as rigid, uncaring, unloving, and detached.

In reality, holding clear boundaries is the opposite; it is about honoring your needs and having self-respect. You can be helpful without becoming helpless. You can still be of service to others without becoming a servant. It means that you understand that there is no excuse for bad behavior and you don't allow people to walk all over you. You respect their needs—they are to respect your needs. It is holding true to your free will and choices and honoring their free will and choices without judgment.

By trying to be understanding and empathic when I was at the party, I lowered my guard. I compromised myself by not being clear. If he asked me a question yet wouldn't let me answer, that was my queue to move on to another conversation with someone else. Instead I forced myself to stay in a situation that made me feel threatened and uncomfortable. I thought I was doing it out of love; instead I stayed out of fear of being judged by him.

Finding the line helped me understand what created an energy tyrant. Close examination of those traits helped me recognize that I too have been an energy tyrant at some points in my life—much to my horror and disgrace—but it was a reality I had to face up to and fix.

Recognizing and acknowledging when I too had been an energy tyrant helped me uncover a little secret that I never knew before. Energy tyrants have absolutely NO idea that they are doing it! Their behavior is the result of unresolved feelings of low self-esteem and a deep-seated, subconscious fear that they are worthless. It is their fear stance—understanding that certainly shifted my perspective. It gave me more compassion and empathy for people who were behaving in energy tyrant mode, but it also gave me the confidence to stand up for myself. It was reassuring to know that there were ways to deal with energy tyrants, but it was also a relief to find out how to overcome the tendency to be one by holding clear boundaries for myself.

Energy tyrants have very poor emotional boundaries and don't know how to respect them in other people. There are two basic types of energy tyrants. The first type of tyrant has little to no self-esteem, so they need to be around other people in order to feel better about themselves. They feed off of other people's energy. It is like their internal emotional battery is running out of power and they need to recharge. The lower the self-esteem, the greater their need to find someone who will let them use their energy field to recharge. Sensitive people are particularly vulnerable to this type of energy tyrant. Their natural empathy and compassion for others makes it difficult for them to feel that it is all right to create any emotional boundaries.

The second type of energy tyrant has such low self-esteem that they need to either bring people down to their level (and feel just as bad about themselves), or they need to tear people down to feel better about themselves.

Both types of energy tyrants are very adept at connecting to you energetically. You don't feel the attachment at first. Until, that is, you start to notice how they literally change before your eyes. The energy tyrant's color changes. They go from looking pale and drawn to glowing with color in their cheeks. They become more animated and joyful. Meanwhile the empathic energy provider starts to wither. Their shoulders begin to sag, their eyes dull, and they try to turn away from the energy tyrant but feel locked into something that has no escape route. Most people are usually unaware that they have been tapped into by an energy tyrant until it is all over. All they know for sure is that they don't feel quite right or they feel demeaned, useless, and powerless.

Hooked, Zapped, and Discharging

Encountering an energy tyrant and being drained is called "getting hooked." The subsequent energy drain from the encounter is called "getting zapped." There are two basic ways to recover from being hooked. The first type of recovery is to have a sudden and totally irrational "blow up" over something minor. These blow ups are usually directed to the one person you are the closest to and feel the safest with. The second type of recovery is to sit down and have a good, roaring cry over what you consider to be nothing. Either method is what I refer to as "discharging." What it does energetically is blast out their hook from your energy field and disconnects you.

Neither method of discharging will endear you to your loved ones if you have been zapped. The discharge appears to be irrational. Suddenly blowing up or crying because your loved one forgot to take out the garbage is a very simple but classic example of a discharge. Any minor or perceived infraction can result in a rather bizarre rage that has everyone feeling battered and bruised for no good reason. The bottom line is nobody understands what the big deal is, least of all you, but there you are crying or carrying on, feeling embarrassed and confused.

Small children who have been zapped, for example, will use this type of discharging technique because their emotional vocabulary hasn't developed enough to accurately describe how they are feeling. Small children are exploring and learning about emotional boundaries, so they are bound to encounter this at school. A sudden bursting into tears or having an angry outburst will help you understand where they are coming from. If you find that this is a regular occurrence in your life or household, it could be a good indicator that you or a loved one is dealing with an energy tyrant at work, school, or through friendships that are not as healthy as they could be.

When I was a child and I had a discharge, my mother would send me to my room to cry it out. I was allowed to leave my room when I was more "civil," as she put it. I could come out and discuss it if I chose to. I sure felt better afterward, but most of the time I was clueless as to why. For this reason, if you find yourself going through a discharge, go to another room. Have a bath, yell at a teddy bear, but don't take it out on loved ones. Be clear about your emotional boundaries and respect theirs.

How to Know You Are Dealing With an Energy Tyrant

Energy tyrants are very adept at finding willing donors. They will attach themselves to anyone who will let them. This is why it is so insidious. You usually don't know it is happening until it is too late. Some energy tyrants actually send out long, octopus like suckers that tap into a person's energy field at their solar plexus chakra. Most energy tyrants are completely unaware that they are doing it, of course, but it is a little disconcerting to watch it happening energetically.

There are numerous ways to know if you have been hooked or zapped by an energy tyrant. You know you are in the presence of an energy tyrant if you feel any of the following symptoms: Your chest feels tight or you are short of breath, you suddenly develop a headache or gut ache, you feel nauseated, your jaw starts to tense up, or you start to feel dizzy, disorientated, and confused and begin to stutter when you speak. The hair on the back of your neck can stand up or make you feel creeped out. You find yourself shifting from foot to foot or suddenly needing to sit down. You have probably been zapped if: You find that you are hovering over the appetizers, returning to the snack bar, or noticing that you are drinking more or ordering doubles. You are at a family dinner, staff meeting, or party and you begin to feel exhausted for no obvious reason and have a desire to be anywhere else but there. You suddenly feel defensive or small in conversation. The person you are speaking with won't let you get a word in edgewise or you suddenly discover that you have a new best friend that follows you around like a lost puppy.

Characteristics of Energy Tyrants

Energy Tyrants can typically have any of the following characteristics: Emotional Enabler—they need constant approval and reassurance; Poor Me—the victim, nothing is my fault; Drama Critic—live from one crisis to another, good at put downs, create problems or blow small issues into emotional fiascoes; Ergo—the egomaniac, all about my way or the highway, always right, cynical, arrogant, and condescending; Chatterbox—they never shut up, every conversation is a breathless encounter, you cannot get a word in edgewise; The Judge— critical of everything and everyone, nothing will ever work, always adept at pointing out all your faults and failures; The Envier—extremely jealous of others, they always find a way to make you feel inferior and show how they are superior, best friend one day, greatest enemy the next. You never know where you stand. Clingons—attach to your field and suck you dry. Little lost puppies that follow you around and always find ways to hang around you.

How to Handle Energy Tyrants

Ask Why?

Ask yourself, "Why do I need them in my life?" What are you hoping they can give you that you can't give yourself? Are you just as needy and afraid as they are? Is this really friendship? Is this how you want to honor yourself? These are hard questions to ask, but they do provide deep insights into what you need or don't need in your life.

Develop Boundaries

Remember there is no excuse for bad behavior. Being present and loving for a friend is one thing; saying no to them and having them respect your wishes is another. A true friend will accept it with grace. An energy tyrant will try to badger you into changing your mind. Being afraid to make them mad disempowers you. You have no control over their behavior, why let them have control over yours?

If you have a friend that constantly takes advantage of you and you are afraid to do anything to stop it, then you are, in effect, supporting their behavior. You are emotionally enabling them by constantly acquiescing to their demands. Your energy fields become intertwined in a self-serving pattern of energy exchange, each setting the other up to be drained and manipulated. It is called codependency. You are both energy tyrants feeding off the other. It's a vicious cycle that serves no one in the end. It is not helping you and it is certainly not teaching them anything. Developing clear emotional boundaries with energy tyrants may be the most courageous, life-affirming thing you ever do. You will be a better person for it.

Walk Away

You always have choice. Never be afraid to make your excuses and leave the room or the conversation. Take a bathroom break. Go to the kitchen and get a glass of water. If you are at a party and are being followed from room to room, don't be afraid to let them know you need to mingle with the other guests. No one wants to be rude, but sometimes you have to be really direct and let him or her know it is time to move on.

Use Energy Tools

Use your cloak of privacy to disappear from them energetically or use the White Light of Protection. It is always the best defense if you know you are going to run into a relative at the family party that loves to tap into you.

Another technique is to imagine there is a mirror between the two of you. See the mirror reflecting their image back to them. As you are doing this, silently repeat "I love you," and direct it to them. Energy tyrants soften when they encounter the energy of love and will start to lose their train of thought, become confused, or stutter. Make your excuses to mingle and move away when they start to falter or lose their train of thought.

It is helpful to remember that anyone who is in energy tyrant mode is suffering from low self-esteem and they are desperate for love and approval. They need allies who will sympathize and justify their existence. If you remain clear about your emotional boundaries and choose not to play in any of their games, they will very quickly lose interest in you. Having firm boundaries will also help you to not feel any guilt. This is because you are recognizing and honoring their choice to stay powerless. If all efforts have been refused, then their choice is clear. You are not responsible for that. You can't help someone who doesn't want to be helped: a tough lesson that we all learn at some point in our lives. Remember everyone has free will and choice. What do you choose?

Once you recognize the symptoms of being sucked dry or manipulated (zapped) and know what the release (discharge) tactics are, you can prevent it from happening in the future. Using your tools will help you to maintain your empathic and compassionate perspective while holding clear boundaries. It will also help you to recognize when a loved one is discharging after an energy tyrant encounter. Don't take it personally but also don't let them make it personal. Call it for what it is. A discharge.

For intuitives, energy tyrants can be particularly draining and difficult to deal with. This is why, as you develop your intuitive abilities, you will understand how important it is to develop strong emotional boundaries. Most of the techniques shared so far will help you to deal with them in more helpful and healthy ways. As you become more adept at using your intuitive abilities, you will find that you also become less attractive to energy tyrants. You have their number, so to speak, and they have no desire to dial in.

Understanding energy tyrants and how they work is also the first step in learning how to establish strong emotional boundaries from a type of energy tyrant that is often overlooked and rarely understood.

10

Emotional Blackmail

There is another type of energy tyrant—the bully. This type of energy tyrant can come in many different forms. The most obvious forms are physical and sexual abuse as well as emotional abuse. However, there is a subset of emotional abuse that is often overlooked. This more elusive form of emotional abuse is what my mom always referred to as "emotional blackmail."

Emotional blackmail is any statement or accusation that undermines, challenges, or dismisses your feelings as being untrue and not believable. It is, at its core, emotional manipulation and sabotage that strikes the heart of your own fears about yourself. It completely undermines you and makes you feel powerless. It can be difficult, if not almost impossible, to feel like you have the right to defend yourself because you are ultimately afraid that what they are saying is really true. Their ego has found a way to make your ego feel even more fearful.

This type of bully—the emotional blackmailer—has come to believe that they are unlovable and have lost all sense of their own self-worth. They will go to great lengths to hide that truth from everyone, including themselves. Their self-esteem has been shattered to such a degree that they'd do anything to get their power back.

They disempower you by using subtle emotional statements to "zap" you into feeling guilty, sad, shameful, or filled with doubt. Its subtle undertones can threaten you with isolation, loneliness, and being unlovable if you don't play along. It can come from individuals, close friends, partners, siblings, or even family members. Family tribes, gangs, or cults can be so fully entrenched in emotional blackmail that they don't even realize they are doing it.

Emotional blackmailers manipulate by using statements like, "You must not love me." Or "If you really loved me." "You are cruel." "You are heartless and unfeeling." "I must not mean anything to you anymore." "So, I'm not good enough for you anymore?" "What's the matter, I'm not smart enough for you?" "You will never amount to anything." "If you leave we will disown you." "If you do this we will never love you again." "I will never speak to you again." "I won't talk to you or listen to you until you apologize." "You aren't smart enough to make it out there." "You can't escape your past." "If you leave, you will have abandoned me again." "You are too stupid to figure this out." The list becomes endless.

Its subtle, pervasive attacks can be from the friend who refuses to be your friend if you don't do what they want; the lover who refuses to love you if you don't do as you are told; the sibling who always brings up that one thing that fills you with shame; the addict who insists that they will change if you help them one more time. These are just a few examples of bully's that use emotional blackmail.

I have often worked with young women who have struggled to break free from emotional blackmail within families or with their partners. I have also worked with people who were caught in vicious divorce proceedings where one partner does everything in their power to make the ex-partner feel guilty or suffer, for the simple reason that they had the nerve to leave.

We are all vulnerable to emotional blackmail. Any statement said to you that makes you feel guilty or forces you to back down or override what you know to be true for you is evidence that you are giving away your power. You are succumbing to your own worst and innermost fears. You are ultimately afraid that what they are saying is really true. It is the classic battle of ego versus love. Their ego can't bear their fear (of loneliness and loss of love) and your ego is afraid (your fear of loneliness and loss of love).

I have found in my own life and in my sessions with clients that there is only one true defense against any of these statements: Whatever the other person says—no matter how they direct it to you, try to make it all about you, try to blame you, or try to threaten you—they are only talking about themselves!

You can defend yourself against emotional blackmail by remembering that they are doing whatever they need to do in order to *project pain away from their egos* and place it on you. They will say or do anything to manipulate you into doing whatever they want because they are afraid of their own truth. You DO NOT have to accept that as your truth! Their fear is not your truth.

One young woman I worked with, Kathy, had tried for years to escape the trap of family poverty and low paying jobs that she grew up with in her family. No one in her family had graduated from high school. She told me, "I was determined to go to college if it was the last thing I ever did." All through high school, Kathy worked several part time jobs to save for college. Her family constantly found reasons to "need that money." If she refused them any amount, they would retaliate by ostracizing her. She was emotionally berated and constantly told that she was a "bad child," or they would tell her "you don't really love us," or "you are selfish and needy." Her dad tried to empty her bank account, but thankfully the bank called to tell her and ask for confirmation, and she was able to stop him. They had a huge fight over it. That's when Kathy started to come and see me.

Kathy was afraid she couldn't take it anymore. She felt that it was only a matter of time before she gave in or her parents found some way to take all the money she had saved for college. She was desperate, afraid, and alone. She had nowhere else left to turn. Her parents even had her boyfriend bugging her for money. He would ask her, "How can you do this to your parents?" Sometimes he would try to borrow money from her as well. When she refused, he would respond with, "I guess you don't love me, either." Kathy told me, "Every time they say that my resolve buckles and I give them some money. I am never going to get into college at this rate. I am losing my dream." Kathy thought her family's behavior was all her fault because she was afraid that her parents were right and that she was being bad, selfish, and unloving.

As I listened to Kathy's story, I knew we were dealing with emotional blackmail from a family tribe level. This meant that there was more than one person involved in blackmailing her. The family had a shared fear belief that they had all accepted to be the truth. I explained all of this to Kathy. I told her, "It's not you, it is their lack of self-esteem stemming from their own fears and lack of self-worth. They are victims of their own fears. They are trying to get you to buy into their beliefs to feel better about themselves. We need to help you understand what it is, what statements they use to enforce it, and how to help you overcome it."

As Kathy and I worked together to identify the emotional blackmail, she realized just how far out into the family tribe their belief system and lack of self-worth was entrenched. Her grandparents, aunts, uncles, and even close family friends were all trapped in this never-ending cycle of poverty. She said to me one day, "Even when my parents had a little money, it wasn't enough, and they would blow it or someone would ask for a loan that never got paid back. It's depressing." As we worked through the sessions, she started to see how even her boyfriend was just another form of her dad. "He does the same thing," she told me. He was always trying to borrow money from her. He started to pressure her to get married and stop taking the pill and get pregnant.

In our sessions together, I helped her to identify the blackmail. We would discuss what fears it created in her and then talk about how to handle the situation or overcome the fear it created in her. We would talk about grounding, listening to her intuition, cloaking, and the White Light of Protection. I taught her how to stay present when she was being taunted or attacked verbally in order to stay detached from their emotional attacks. She learned how to not take responsibility for how they felt or reacted. Instead, she learned how to let them rant and just wait until it was over. Then she would say, "I am sorry you feel that way. I love you," and leave for her bedroom or go and stay with a friend. Within a short period of time, Kathy become more skilled at seeing how their fears were making them feel small and how they were trying to feed off of her and disempower her.

One day she came home from working a double shift to find that her parents had moved her boyfriend into her room.

Her dad told her, "It's time you settled down and had a baby."

She told me, "I couldn't believe it. I just stood there looking at them. I couldn't breathe. I was speechless."

Kathy said, "What did me in was the look on my boyfriend's face. He stood there with this stupid grin on his face like he had won."

"That's when I knew he didn't love me. He was using me. My parents were using me. I couldn't take it anymore. I picked up my purse and walked out," she said. "I felt so calm and peaceful when I did. When I walked outside I felt like I could breathe for the first time in my life." Kathy had tears streaming down her face as she spoke, but boy she looked empowered!

Moving out didn't stop all the emotional blackmail, but it gave her the distance she needed to meet her own goals. She couch surfed for a while until she could find a room in a boarding house. Her parents would call her up and berate her. She learned to stop picking up the phone when her parents called. After she was settled into her new place and felt more grounded, she would get in touch. If her parents used any emotional blackmail statements, she would take a deep breath and realize they were only verbalizing their own fears. Kathy learned how to listen and not engage or defend. Her boyfriend tried to contact her for a while but she learned to not respond to any of his messages. She deleted all his e-mails, texts, and voicemails without listening to or reading them. We continued to work together helping her to discover her own sense of self-worth while maintaining that inner power. We connected her to her intuitive gifts and showed her how to tap into the inner calm. By doing so, she learned how to manage the ego voice that wanted to buy into the emotional blackmail.

Kathy finally realized her dream and got into a good college and moved away. A few years later I got a call from her. She told me that she had met a really nice guy at college. They helped each other finish school and they both found great jobs after they graduated. They were married now and expecting their first baby. She told me, "While I am off on maternity leave, I am going to start my Masters." She told me, "Someday, I want to get my doctorate. My husband is all for it. I am living my dream. Thank you."

How to Handle Emotional Blackmail

Recognize the Blackmail

The first step in handling emotional blackmail is recognizing and acknowledging that you are being emotionally blackmailed. It can come from anyone—there are no exceptions. If what is being said to you makes you feel powerless, weak, tearful, guilty, afraid, or sad—and that makes you break down, give in, or forces you to do something against your better judgment—then you are dealing with an emotional blackmailer. If you feel uneasy, uncertain, hesitant, or uncomfortable, then your intuition is trying to tell you that what they are saying isn't true for you.

You may have to accept the fact you have given in for years or tolerated their behavior because you love them, but deep down you feel angry, miserable, and guilty. Now that you know, you are ready to face the facts and deal with it. Recognizing that your denial and excuses have only taken you so far will help you start reclaiming your power and self-respect. It is time to take back the life you deserve and dream about.

Learning how to say no will be one of the most powerful things you can do. Learning how to say no and mean no can be a challenge. It takes courage to face your own fears and move past the little ego voice that keeps you small. Remember there is no excuse for bad behavior, and that doesn't just mean from others, it means treating yourself with respect and honoring your own dreams and feelings. No one can get to you unless you let them. The hardest but best part of saying no is understanding that it is, and always will be, a complete sentence. No explanation is required.

Breathe

When the attack happens, focus in on your breath and wait for them to stop. Breathe in and breathe out.

Ground

Use your one word to go into your Vertical Axis.

Protect

Use your one word to go into the White Light of Protection. Use your cloak any time you know you are going to be around them.

Listen but Do Not Engage

Listen to what they are saying but do not react. This is important: *do not argue, react, or engage.* You will be tempted to because you will be upset or shocked by what they are saying to you. Be prepared for that. As hard as it is to listen, you need to hear what they are saying so that you can work on what is making *you* feel powerless. Recognize that anything they say, *they are only talking about themselves.* They will do their utmost to try to find a way to make you believe what they are saying. No matter what, *please* remember that whatever they are saying is their truth—not yours. Keep reminding yourself of that.

If you try to defend yourself or correct what they are saying, you will only get trapped into an argument that you cannot win. It only makes them that much more determined to make you accept what they are saying. When they have stopped talking or you can't listen to another word, say either, "I am sorry you feel that way, I love you," or "I am sorry you believe that is true, I love you."

Leave

After the encounter is over, leave the room, leave the house, drive away, stay at a friend's house, or go for a walk. Take a bath (lock the door so that they can't corner you in the tub). Hang up the phone or delete the e-mail or voicemail. (Unless of course you are involved in a court case or divorce and need evidence. In that case save a copy, but don't read it if you don't have to.) If you are in the car and can't leave, ask them to pull over at the nearest restaurant or gas station. If they won't stop the car, then get out at a stoplight near a store or gas station when it is safe to do so. Then call a cab or have a friend come and get you. If they are following you, go to a public place, call a friend or the police, and stay put until they arrive and walk into the building and escort you out.

Journal

Write down what they said. Write down why you think it is true. Then ask yourself if it is really true or if you are afraid it is true. Write down how it makes you feel. Emotional blackmailers are going for the jugular. They strike at the heart of your emotions. I can guarantee you that what they are saying to you has either caught you off guard or came out of left field. They will either want something, need something, or they are trying to get you to do something you know is not right. They are looking for the one thing that they know will make you *feel* your deepest fear—that you are not really loved or you are unlovable. With that comes a fear of isolation from friends, family, or a co-worker.

For Kathy, her journal helped her understand what the emotional blackmail looked like in her family. She would bring the statement into session and we would work together to see what was really going on beneath the surface. Once we isolated her fears that were triggered as a result of the emotional blackmail, we would take the statement, flip it around, and examine it from another angle.

For example: Whenever Kathy got a promotion or a raise at work and tried to share it with her parents, they would respond with, "You think you're better than us now?" The trigger for Kathy was her fear of bragging and making her parents feel bad. We would look at her fear of bragging. Kathy remembered when she was six years old she told her parents she got an A in a spelling test. She was so proud. Her parents laughed at her and told her to stop bragging. She was devastated. She stopped studying for her spelling tests and started to fail. Her teacher pulled her aside one day and asked her why she did so well in the beginning and was failing now. Kathy told her teacher what happened when she did well. Her teacher was very smart, and said, "You continue to study and don't tell you parents how well you are doing. They can't handle success." Kathy had forgotten about that story until we looked at her fear of bragging. Kathy stopped telling her parents about promotions or raises. She realized they couldn't handle it because it made them feel insecure. Her teacher was right. They didn't know how to handle success. That helped Kathy feel more confident. She was able to observe her parents more closely after that. What she discovered really surprised her. Her dad couldn't read. She realized her mom read everything to her dad. She said it was so subtle how they did that. "I never realized how he even made me read things to him if we were in a store," she said.

It's All About Them

Once you are able to recognize the fear that emotional blackmail creates in you, then you can flip it around. You can see how they are actually using emotional blackmail to hide the fact that any emotional blackmail statement is really all about them. It doesn't matter how they say it, frame it, phrase it, deny it, or twist it, they are *always* talking about their own fears. If they say, "You don't love me," what they are really saying is, "I don't love ME." If they say, "You don't care about me," flip it and see what they are really saying: "I don't care about me."

"You never listen to me"	"I can't hear myself"
"You are selfish"	"I think I am selfish"
"You never loved me"	"I never loved myself"

Whenever Kathy's parents asked her for money, it made her feel guilty if she refused. Journaling helped her to remember an incident that happened when she was sixteen. She had announced to her parents at supper one day that she had decided she wanted to go to college. Her dad looked at her and got really mad. He started to yell at her and tell her she was too stupid for college. "How are you going to pay for that, smarty pants?" he asked. She told him she got a part-time job and she was saving up. "That made him even madder," she said. "He didn't know I had a bank account."

Writing out the story helped Kathy to recognize that she was afraid she was a fool and that her dream wasn't realistic. She was afraid that her dad was right. She recognized that her family wasn't that well-off and they could use the extra money for food, rent, clothes, gas, or repairs. She felt guilty and thought she should share and help out. When we examined her guilt and fear around being a fool, it helped her to see that both her parents had jobs but never had any money left at the end of the week. Her dad would buy beer before he would part with a dime for groceries. Her mom paid for everything out of her paycheck. They fought about money all the time. They didn't know how to handle their money and were too afraid to learn how. She started to understand that they kept themselves powerless around money. They didn't need to be poor. That was their choice and she didn't need to buy into it or believe it was the only way to cope. If she tried to help out, it was never enough. They didn't appreciate it and would ridicule her even more. All she could do was love them and not fall into the same trap.

Move On

Once you start to recognize the pattern of emotional blackmail, you will have to decide what to do about it. This can be tough and take a lot of courage. If you are in a marriage where your partner is using these tactics to control you, there is some work ahead to help you regain your self-esteem and self-respect. Once that happens, the dynamic of the relationship will either heal or dissolve.

By the time Kathy had finally left for college, she had learned how to look at the emotional blackmail from a different perspective. She didn't buy into it anymore. She realized that it was okay to develop clear boundaries and be aware of when her family tried to find other ways to manipulate her. She used the tools I gave her. Grounding, white light, cloaking, and cutting fear cords all helped her cope and get on with the rest of her life. It gave her a level of self-confidence she never knew she had.

Anyone can become an emotional blackmailer. I am loath to admit it, but I became one when I was newly married. I didn't realize it at the time, but Bert sure knew something wasn't right. He travelled all the time and was rarely home. I couldn't wait for him to come home on weekends. When he did finally come home, I always managed to find something to pick a fight over. After several months of this he had enough. He talked to our minister who suggested that I needed to see a therapist. When Bert came home and told me what they had discussed, I hit the roof! I could not believe what he was saying to me. I accused him of turning against me and betraying my confidence. I pulled out all the stops. I screamed, wailed, and cried. My husband very wisely sat there and waited for me to cool down and get it off my chest. When I was done, he looked at me and said, "I love you. We are in this marriage for the long haul, but you need help and I can't help you." He left the room and let me cry it out. I was stunned. No one had ever talked to me like that in my entire life.

I cried for days. He made an appointment with a therapist anyway. He drove me to my first appointment. I cried all the way there. He just kept telling me he loved me. By the time I got into the therapist office, I was one very angry woman. I had pretty much decided that I was ready to walk away from the marriage.

I can tell you that seeing a therapist was one of the best things that ever happened to me. I am so grateful my husband loved me that much that he made me go. My therapist helped me to understand that I was taking all of my fears out on Bert. I was young, immature, and away from home for the first time in my life. I had no friends, a job I hated, and I felt lost and afraid. I was left alone in a strange city all by myself for days on end. Somewhere along the line I had lost all of my self-confidence. I didn't recognize the fear in me, let alone know how to name it. Having someone guide me through the fear gave me the tools I needed to face them in myself. I stopped taking my fears out on my husband and learned to take ownership of my own feelings. I also needed to take a long, hard look at when I had been emotionally blackmailed as a child. I grew up in a very dysfunctional home, and there are still times when I look back and realize what a miracle it was that I managed to get out. It was hard to recognize and accept the amount of emotional blackmail my mom had been subjected to in her lifetime.

The truth of the matter was my husband couldn't heal my past. I was the only one who could look at what happened to me in my childhood and accept the level of woundedness I was raised in. That was really hard to accept. Eventually I was able to see how my past had made me stronger. I became more compassionate, tolerant, understanding, and less judgmental. I created strong boundaries around my family relationships and stopped buying into the blackmail. I no longer apologized for what I knew was my own truth. I started doing what was right for me and my family.

There are still the odd times when I need to be reminded that I am falling into an old pattern. If I am upset, my husband will let me rant and then he will say, "Okay, now that you have that off your chest, what's really bugging you?" It always makes me laugh, but I get the point.

Dealing with sick relatives, teenagers with addictions, or toxic friendships each have their own challenges. Using these survival tactics can help you maneuver through the emotional turmoil and hopefully find some solutions. Sometimes all you can do is listen and walk away. Other situations will require tough love and a refusal to be trapped. Seeking the help of a qualified therapist might be your best option. Everyone has to make a choice. We don't always like or approve of a loved one's choices. We don't know why a soul chooses the path that it does. Learning how to deal with emotional blackmail may take some time. The important thing is to learn how to stand your ground, live your own truth, and listen to your inner calm. You are divinely loved and have the power of choice. You don't need to buy into being bullied by an emotional blackmailer. Recognize their lack of self-love and powerlessness. Embrace your self-love and be empowered.

It is how you become the master of your own dance while utilizing your intuitive gifts and staying connected to the inner calm.

Part IV
Clearing
Your Energy

Everything is connected. Just as we are all drops of water in the ocean of life, we are all part of the larger divine. Every thought and feeling we have creates a vibration which moves out in waves from our aura. These waves of energy move outward and they begin to form energetic connections with other people. These connections create something called "etheric cords." These cords are the subtle energetic pathways of shared feelings and emotions.

There are three primary etheric cords that enter the body. The first is the "soul cord," which is our connection to universal divine. The second is a "love cord," which carries the vibration of love. The third etheric cord carries fear vibrations and is called a "fear cord." There are many different forms of fear cords, all of which are an energetic nuisance that can create additional stress and anxiety. Fear cords can also affect your health and sense of well-being. Removing them is easy, therapeutic, and incredibly liberating.

Just as energy moves between two people creating cords, energy also fills up space in and around the objects of our homes. These are called energy imprints, and they can also have a direct impact on your family harmony and the health and happiness of your home. They are like an emotional smog, completely unseen but intuitively felt. We will explore how to clear your space and fill it with the energy of divine love and protection. You will also learn how to create a dome of protection for your home and property.

After you have cleared all the fear cords and balanced your home and property, there still remains the memory of past hurts and traumatic events. Is there a way to heal toxic energy that has already been released in the past? How does one channel the energy created from a toxic relationship or situation into something more positive and helpful? We will explore the power of a new technique called "energetic do-overs." We will also explore the process of forgiveness.

11

Cutting Cords

We are in contact with other people all day, every day. Whether it be in person, on the phone, or over the internet, we still connect to other people energetically. After a while all that energy contact with other people starts to build up on the outer edges of our fields. Remember static cling? Well, this is the same thing. A little hand lotion gets rid of static cling on your panty hose, and a little angel intervention goes a long way to taking care of the static cling in your energy field.

As you develop your intuitive abilities, you will start to feel how these ties can either bind or build. How these cords are created, how they impact our lives, and how to manage or remove them is a fascinating aspect of learning how to dance with your ego and find your inner calm.

In her book, *Light Emerging*, Barbara Ann Brennan states that "any action we do is preceded by thought and feeling that can be seen in the auric field before we follow through with the action. In other words we do things energetically before we do them physically" (1993, 182).

When two people interact, their thoughts and feelings are being transmitted in their auras. This information is exchanged energetically through etheric cords. These energy cords can be uplifting and positive (love) or they can be manipulative, controlling, and draining (fear). It all depends on the reason or intent behind what created them in the first place.

3 Kinds of Energy Cords

In my professional experience, there are three types of energy cords created by the body and its energy field: love cords, fear cords, and the soul cord. The soul cord is divinely generated and is our connection to God, the Divine or spiritual consciousness. Love cords form any time there is a relationship between people or pets we love and care about. Fear cords are created whenever there is any kind of fear. Fear cords can form when we are feeling like we are being attacked and need to defend ourselves or need to control or manage someone's behavior or reaction.

The Soul Cord

The soul cord is also referred to as the silver cord of life. It is our direct connection to the Divine (God) or Spirit. This spiritual connection enters into the body through the belly button. Energy flows down from the heavens through the silver cord into our body and enters into an energy center called the "hara" (2002, 107). Located just below the belly button, the hara is described by Graf von Durckheim[4] as the "original life center of man" (107). From the hara, this spiritual energy is distributed out into our chakras through an energy channel system called the "nadi." The nadi is like an energetic nervous system that feeds our subtle energy system.

Proof that these silver cords of life do in fact exist comes from thousands of stories relayed by people who have had either a near-death experience or an out of body experience where they recount following the silver cord back to their bodies.

My mother had a near-death experience when she hemorrhaged while giving birth to my older sister. She remembers floating above her body and watching the doctor trying to save her. She remembers her spirit rolling over and going up through the ceiling into the light. As she ascended, there were angels who greeted her. She told me, "I had never felt such complete and utter peace and love like that ever." She

---

4. Graf von Durckheim (1896–1988) was a German diplomat, psychotherapist, and
   Zen master.

was told she couldn't stay and had to return to her body. She remembers begging them to let her stay. The angels said her time was not over and that there were five things that would happen in her lifetime. With a great deal of sadness and despair, she returned to her body, something that took her years to overcome. My mother said, "I followed the cord back to my body and re-entered. I never got over the weight of my body again. I always felt like I was in a wet suit three sizes too small." She also told me that of the five things she had been told by the Angels, three had come true so far. "I have never feared dying ever since," she told me.

I was always so intrigued by that story and I never forgot it. Imagine my surprise when I started to see and feel soul cords when I started working with clients in my healing practice. They look and feel like umbilical cords that shimmer with a silvery, blue light. Soul cords cannot be removed, but I will touch them when I am in the process of explaining to clients where they are and why they exist. Clients often report to me that they can sense it when I touch them. They express a sense of wonder when they feel it, finding it to be very reassuring to know that they actually do exist. I tell my clients that my angel guardians say our belly buttons are a physical reminder that the soul cord is there. That always makes my clients smile.

Love Cords

Love cords are formed between parents, children, spouses, pets, and anyone else that has a significant impact in our lives. They are located in the heart area. They can be big or small depending on the intensity of the connection with someone we love. Love cords between a mother and her child are generally very large, as are love cords between two people who love and cherish each other. If we lose a loved one, it can be a heart wrenching experience because the love cord is severed quickly. Clients will often report that after the death of a spouse or parent, it feels hard to breathe or they feel hollow inside The loss of a child will always create this type of deep void in the parents because they are physically feeling the energetic loss of the love cord with their child. If the loss of a loved one has been particularly tragic or unexpected, I will often find that there is a hole or indentation at or near the heart chakra that can change the body's physical appearance.

I once worked with a gentleman who developed a concave rib cage after he lost his wife in a car accident. They were childhood sweethearts and she was the love of his life. When she died, he said, "I knew something was wrong the minute it happened. I was asleep when all of a sudden I felt like something had been pulled out of my chest. I sat straight up from a deep sleep and started gasping and coughing. I was terrified. I thought I was having a heart attack. I couldn't catch my breath. Then I suddenly realized I couldn't feel my wife energetically anymore. I knew then and there, at that moment, something horrible had happened to her and she was gone. The phone rang five minutes later. It was the police calling to say she had been killed by a drunk driver."

He didn't notice the physical change to his rib cage until a few weeks later. "I was getting dressed and the sun was shining. I caught a glimpse of my profile in the mirror. My chest looked totally different. It looked like it had collapsed in on itself. I was shocked," he said. "But I understood. Losing her was more than I could bear and my body reflected that. It's no wonder I couldn't breathe properly." Energy work repaired his damaged heart chakra and the indentation to his rib cage disappeared within a few months.

Fear Cords

Fear cords, on the other hand, can be found anywhere on the body, front and back. They can be created between anyone you are in contact with. Whether it be in person, on the phone, over the Internet, or whether you are simply thinking angry or fearful thoughts about someone, fear cords are an energetic nuisance that are easily made and they are incredibly disruptive. I know how easy it is to make them because I still do it all the time with my own children, even though I know better and try very hard not to. Thank goodness they are easy to remove!

Fear cords can also develop in relationships where one person has a need to manage and control outcomes. People who are rageaholics, for example, radiate fear cords that shoot out and attach to anybody.

Energy tyrants generate fear cords that literally seek out other sources of energy and use them to connect to other people energetically. If we are caught up in the crazy ego dance of making up fearful, angry thoughts, plots, or defenses in our minds, we create energy threads that spin out from our fields and carry the energy of that thought or feeling outwards. These energy threads then "target" the person we are thinking about. Once that thread "hits" their field, it will either die off because you forgot all about it or it will continue to grow and develop. Having "mind fights" with someone will always generate fear cords that grow and develop the more you feed it with fear. Struggling with manufactured fear created by the ego will also generate fear cords. Feed the fear long enough and it will become a well-developed fear cord that affects you and the party you are upset with. Any type of fear cord will start to restrict and hamper the other person's energy, as well as your own.

A buildup of fear cords that are filled with negative ego intents can be a major cause of stress, burnout, and chronic fatigue. I have uncovered fear cords in clients who are suffering from post-traumatic stress disorder (PTSD) that are large enough to have literally caused them to still be energetically connected to the original location where the trauma has occurred. I find this to be especially true when working with victims of war and veterans. It is not uncommon to have veterans remark that they always feel like they left a piece of themselves behind and why they have so much trouble returning home. Fear cords are really much more common than people believe.

I have found fear cords can be anything from thin whispers that look like and feel like sewing thread to massive shapes the size of a huge tree trunk. They can feel like twisted forms of rage and are so solid in nature that you can actually feel the texture in your hands energetically. The bigger the cord, the longer it has been there and the more it has been fed by both parties who are locked in a disagreement of some sort. They are always present when there has been a power struggle between two people, especially between a parent and a child.

What never ceases to amaze me in my practice is how much healing can transpire when fear cords have been removed. I have seen instances where two people who have not talked to each other for years suddenly find that they can barely remember what caused the friction in the first place. Clients have told me stories of finally being able to be in the same room with an estranged parent after years of hardly being able to look at them. It didn't mean that anyone had changed, per se, it just meant that the client realized that being angry with the parent wasn't the solution anymore. Parents were finally able to come to terms with a child's addiction and move forward with their lives, despite the child's tragic choices in life.

Healing from deep-seated grief over the loss of a partner or child has also been quite common once fear cords were removed. Conflicts between siblings that had been going on since childhood settled down and there was a sense of order and peace in the family again. Couples who bickered constantly found themselves to be more understanding and compassionate toward each other. Women who were being abused by their spouses finally found the courage to leave and start a fresh life. I have even seen instances where those involved in bitter divorce cases have suddenly been able to resolve their differences and reach an amicable resolution once fear cords were removed between all the parties involved, including the lawyers and judges. The list is endless. Is it the cure for all emotional distress? No, but fear cord removals do go a long, long way to clearing energetic pathways that can block the path back to a place of love and harmony. Even if that path means finally finding the strength to leave an impossible situation to finally be free to live life on your own terms.

Cutting Fear Cords

There are several methods for cutting loose from fear cords. All are very easy and effective. For the everyday static cling, I like to work with Archangel Michael, but you can use any Archangel you like. If you don't like the idea of working with an angel, then by all means work with God, Jesus, Mother Mary, Buddha, Mohammed, or another ascended master that you feel most connected to spiritually. All of these ascended beings are here to be of service and are happy to help in any way they can. "Ask and it shall be given" is always a good reminder.

Remember though: they have to be asked in order to help. They will always honor your free will and cannot, nor will they, interfere with your choices in life, in any way.

The thing to remember is that only fear cords can be cut. Angels can only cut and clear out static, fear cords, and negative energy. They *cannot* and *will not* remove love. Love is a gift from the Divine and it stands for everything they are and believe in. Be aware that when you say you want to clear static and fear cords from everybody, you mean *everybody*, even the people you love. This is because you are also purposely releasing any fear that you may have unintentionally created with loved ones.

This particular fear-cord cutting exercise is very powerful and easy to use. I recommend that it be done daily to clear all the static cling that has gathered throughout your day from any conversations or interactions you have had with anyone. I tell my clients that gathering this type of fear is like not dusting your house for a year. You get used to the mess but it doesn't look pretty, and it's not comfortable to be around. Clearing out this kind of static and fear will keep the love channels open—not clogged down with unnecessary fear and anxiety.

If you choose to work with Archangel Michael, he is the patron saint of protection who offers courage, peace, and safety to all who call upon him. He releases us from fear and doubt and helps to clear negativity. He is one of the most powerful archangels.

When you work with Archangel Michael to do the fear cord cutting, he will use a great big sword that sparkles with a translucent, blue light. As he passes the sword through the energy field to clear all the static and fear cords, it always reminds me of what a light saber from *Star Wars* sounds like. After he is done, say thank you or amen. You will feel much lighter and happier afterward.

🪷 Technique 🪷
Fear Cord Cutting

Close your eyes and go into your Vertical Axis, either using the full Vertical Axis meditation or using your one word. (The Vertical Axis Technique, Step-by-Step, page 93)

Silently call in Archangel Michael. Imagine or pretend that he appears before you and see him smiling at you. As he stands before you, feel him surrounding you with his love and blessings.

Ask the following: "Archangel Michael, please cut and clear all static and fear cords with everyone I have been in contact with on this day."

Then imagine or pretend he waves his blue sword all over your body and energy field from front to back. As he does so, all the static, fear cords, and negative energy you have encountered throughout the day are removed from your entire aura, front and back. When he is done, he will stand back. Thank him or say amen.

The entire procedure should only take about five seconds—Archangels, ascended masters, and teachers are all pretty efficient. If it is taking longer than that, then you are trying too hard or are too afraid you are doing it incorrectly. Not to worry. You have asked and he has given, whether you can feel it or not.

Clients who did the Fear Cord Cutting Technique on a daily basis found that work was much easier and less stressful. They felt calmer and more relaxed. It was helping them sleep better and they found they weren't tossing and turning all night worrying about things or replaying mind arguments. I often hear clients remark that cord cutting on a regular basis helped them see when their egos were looking for something to be fearful about, and then they were able to stop it. I call it "nipping drama in the bud."

Those of my clients who were particularly sensitive to being out in public, and who had found crowds overwhelming, found doing this technique on a daily basis helped them overcome feeling intimidated or overwhelmed. They found that going out in public was more comfortable and easy. For many it was a new found freedom.

Adjusting Cord Cutting Techniques for Children

Mothers would ask me if they could use this cord cutting technique with their young children. I didn't see why not. It had always worked well when I shared it with older children and teenagers. Very young children, who are already very open to their intuitive abilities, found working with angels a little too intimidating, though. That is until one young mother came up with a brilliant solution. She had two lovely, intuitive children who were amazing. They could sense and feel everything going on around them. Many days were lost at school due to phantom tummy aches and constant headaches. We both knew what the problem was. These gifted children where feeling everything in their environment but didn't know how to discern what was theirs and what belonged to the other children. The end result is that they would bring it all home, all that energy still sitting there in their fields, and they didn't know how to let it go.

I couldn't figure out how to help these gifted children so that they wouldn't feel frightened by cord cutting and removing energetic static from their fields. Until, that is, the mother was shopping one day and saw a feather duster for sale. She thought, "Why can't I dust off the static?" Every night before her children go to bed, she dusts off the day from their fields. The children LOVE it! It has eliminated the majority of their phantom tummy aches, and headaches are becoming a thing of the past. If school is particularly challenging that day, they will ask for a dust-down before supper.

As I started to share this technique with other families and young children, they would report back how they had developed their own versions to dust off their children's emotional static. One mother said they use her child's favorite stuffed toy bunny rabbit to do the dusting. If they try to use another stuffed animal, her daughter says, "The bunny does it better." She just laughed. She said her partner thinks it is a little weird, but their daughter seems to sleep better at night, so who is to say it is wrong? Sometimes you just have to roll with it. These children are extremely intuitive, and they have a lot to teach us.

Toxic Relationships

Cutting loose also means knowing when to walk away when a relationship becomes toxic. This can happen if there is an extreme difference of opinion that develops between two parties who disagree on a course of action. Or there can be ego entanglements because behavior has become abusive. One person feels used and underappreciated, while the other person, who's imposing their will, becomes more demanding. These are the classic energetic power plays that are often the end result between energy tyrants and those enduring years of emotional blackmail.

Toxic relationships can also develop in the workplace because someone feels the need to assert their authority in order to feel better about themselves. I have personally found myself in several workplace situations where this was the case. One person is making everybody's life miserable because they need to feel better about themselves.

High turnover rates in companies are often an indication that someone in the office is making things as difficult as possible for the staff. Situations such as these create a lot of unnecessary anxiety and fear, and they reduce company morale. It takes its toll on employees and their families. It never ceases to amaze me that corporations don't conduct cost studies to determine their losses and lost productivity because of stress leave and constant retraining, simply because everybody is afraid to face the one person who is creating chaos.

If you find yourself in a toxic relationship, use this exercise and personalize it to address your personal situation.

Cutting Loose a Toxic Relationship with Archangel Michael

Close your eyes and go into your Vertical Axis, either using the full Vertical Axis meditation or using your one word. (The Vertical Axis Technique, Step-by-Step, page 93)

> *Imagine or pretend that you are standing in heaven. You feel calm and peaceful here. You feel totally safe and surrounded by divine love. Silently call in Archangel Michael. Imagine or pretend that he appears before you, and you see him smiling at you and surrounding you with his love and blessings.*
>
> *Ask: "Archangel Michael, please cut, remove, and release all static and all fear cords between me and [_____]. I ask*

that this cord and static be removed at all levels, in all time, in all forms, and in all realities. I ask that this static and fear cord between us be completely dissolved and transformed into love and light for the good of all. Amen"

Then imagine or pretend he takes his blue sword and cuts the fear cord between the two of you. Then he reaches out and gently pulls the fear cord out from your body. Then imagine or pretend that he then turns to the other person and removes the other end of the fear cord from them. As he does so, all the fear and negative energy you have encountered from this person is totally and completely removed from both of your auras, front and back, and immediately transformed into love and light for the good of all.

When all the fear energy is removed, Archangel Michael then holds out his hands and fills your field and their field with divine love and light to make you both whole again. When he is done, he stands back. Now see the other person being gently guided back to their body by a band of angels. Now feel yourself being gently guided back to your body by Archangel Michael. Thank him or say amen.

Slowly open your eyes and look around the room. Take a few moments to journal any thoughts, feelings, or insights that you received.

The Ultimate Fear Cord Cutting

Some conflicts in life run deeper than the negative energy we pick up after daily encounters. Whenever there has been punishing trauma, such as abuse (physically, mentally, emotionally, or spiritually) or a long-term toxic relationship with a parent, spouse, sibling, colleague, or friend that has left you almost depleted of any self-esteem, this technique may give you the freedom to move on with the rest of your life. I find this technique to be extremely powerful and healing. I have also been witness to deep healing after assisting in cord removals after stalkings, attempted murder, or in situations that have resulted in PTSD from soldiers returning from war and combat.

I have also witnessed dramatic physical healing in situations that were the result of physical abuse or rape. Chronic pelvic inflammation, infections, or hip problems literally disappeared overnight. One client of mine was able to cancel a hip replacement operation after we dealt with the fear and trauma she suffered as the result of date rape that had occurred twenty years earlier. Some clients reported that their joints stopped aching after doing the Ultimate Fear Cord Cutting. I have also been witness to the physical and emotional healing that occurs when cords are cut as the result of a traumatic birthing experience. Mother and child are finally able to bond or an episiotomy that refuses to heal suddenly clears up. The list is endless.

❧ Technique ❧
The Ultimate Cord Cutting

To do this technique, it is recommended that you find a quiet place to be alone and not interrupted. You will need a candle, some Kleenex, your journal, and a pen. Think about the person you want to do the cord cutting with. Think about all the issues you have with this person. Think about the pain it has caused you. Write down what you are hoping to accomplish by releasing this person into the hands of the Divine.

If you feel afraid, ask Archangel Michael or the Lord Jesus to stand with you and surround you with their divine love and protection. Remember: whatever has happened, you have survived. They are no longer able to touch you or threaten you. You are a testament to the courage that was needed to survive, and you are standing here now, in all your power, reclaiming your life. What has happened is in the past. You are divinely loved, divinely guided, and divinely protected.

Light a candle and say a prayer of love and guidance. For example, you could say the Lord's Prayer or use the Prayer of Protection.

Prayer of Protection

Dear Archangel Michael, please surround me with your love and protection. Guide and protect me at all levels of my being: physically, emotionally, mentally, and spiritually in all time, in all forms, and in all dimensions. Amen.

Close your eyes and go into your Vertical Axis either using the full Vertical Axis meditation or using your one word. (The Vertical Axis Technique, Step-by-Step, page 93)

Now imagine or pretend that you are standing in heaven. It is calm and peaceful here. You feel totally safe and surrounded by divine love. Silently call in Archangel Michael. Imagine or pretend that he appears before you, and you see him smiling at you and surrounding you with his love and blessings. Now call in the person you wish to cut cords with.
Now ask:

I, [_____], do cut and sever all cords, ties, and attachments with [_____] and all their fear and all my fear. I cut and sever all cords, ties, and attachments with all the fear that I have as a result of them and all the fear they have as a result of me at all levels, in all dimensions, in all time, in all forms, in all realities, and in all lifetimes of my being.

All contracts, bond, oaths, vows, promises, alliances, and agreements known and unknown in all time, space, and matter are now null and void. I ask that the aspect of myself that allowed for this cord and attachment to be created now be made null and void and sent to my higher self for healing. I ask that any energy released be transformed in love and light for the good of all. I ask that we both be filled with the love of God and divine light for healing. Amen.

This procedure will have a profound effect on your relationship with the person you have just disconnected from. They will know at some intuitive level that something has shifted. You will find that your response to them is easier and more peaceful.

I often hear clients say that for the first time in years they were able to have a civil conversation with their mom or dad. One client told me that the phone was ringing as soon as she arrived home after we did the Ultimate Cord Cutting Technique. She told me:

Sure enough it was mummy on the phone. She was looking to start an argument with me again, and for the first time ever I didn't react. I had absolutely no desire to engage in an argument with her. I stood there and patiently listened to her rant at me on the phone, and all I could say was, "Gee, Mom, I'm sorry you feel that way," then I said goodbye and hung up. For the first time in years I felt totally free of all her drama. I realized that it wasn't mine to own. She just needed to be mad all the time and it wasn't my fault. After I put the phone down I started laughing. I finally understood that I could still love her and not have to fix her. It made all the difference in the world. I was no longer attached to her drama.

She smiled at me. She said, "My husband is so relieved he doesn't have to deal with the constant tension between us anymore!"

Other clients of mine who were dealing with ex-lovers who just wouldn't leave them alone also said the same thing after doing the cord cutting. One client, who I will call Miranda, said, "I did what you advised me to do. I removed all traces of him from my phone, computer, and home using the Space Clearing Exercise (page 203). Then I did the Ultimate Fear Cord Cutting Technique, and within a day or two, he stopped trying to contact me. It was like he disappeared. I felt like I could breathe again." Another client of mine who was in a similar situation with an ex-boyfriend told me, "A few days after I did the Ultimate Fear Cord Cutting Technique, I happened to run into him at a restaurant. When I saw him, I felt nothing, and he acted like he didn't know who I was. It was hilarious. After three years of fighting, to be free of him, that's all it took."

I'm not going to pretend that this cord cutting technique is a cure-all, but if you find yourself in a situation that is toxic or you are feeling bullied and intimidated, it is well worth the effort. Fear cords carry a lot of very negative energy. If you don't want it in your life, remove it. You have the power and the right. It will open up new, more positive possibilities in your life and dramatically reduce the stress you are dealing with in this type of situation. Never forget the power you have to manage and control what is happening in your life. Our bodies have such an amazing ability to recover and heal when we give ourselves permission to remove these negative energy patterns or traumas.

Developing a daily practice of clearing out the static and cutting the negative fear cords with Archangel Michael goes a long way to teaching you to manage your own energy. It also helps you to stop feeling like you need to carry or manage someone else's life. After all, emotions are just energy, too. Form always follows thought. Add in the spiritual law of "like attracts like," and you can quickly see where negative energy can attract things into your life that are not healthy. The beauty of all of this is knowing that fear cords are energy just like everything else in life. Knowing that you have the power and ability to clear your aura of any type of fear is incredibly liberating. Learning how you can also clear your space of negative and ungrounded energy is the next step.

12

Cleaning Up the Energy in Your Space

In ballroom dancing there is nothing worse than a dirty dance floor. My husband and I attended a wedding once where the floor was so dirty that you actually stuck to it! It reminded me that the same thing can happen in life. We can get stuck in our lives and that can make it difficult to move, let alone dance to the music of life. Ballroom dancing, for example, is about style, form, and movement. Dancers need to hear the beat, know the correct style of dance, hold the right form, and move in harmony with everyone else on the floor. Get it wrong and you end up missing the beat and going against the flow.

It never dawned on me that my home could be a major contributor to stress and anxiety. It was a lesson my husband and I learned in a very unusual way. It saved our marriage and our careers, and it brought a level of happiness and success that we never thought possible. It also gave us deeper respect and understanding of our spiritual connection to the Divine. All of this came from a simple dinner invitation that I almost refused to accept.

My Husband was attending a conference in Florida one year when he ran into Ted, an old friend of his from college. They worked in different industries, so they had lost touch over the years. Bert told Ted things hadn't gone so well for us over the years as a result of all the corporate restructuring and downsizing we had been through with our careers. Ted listened intently and then suggested we get together for dinner. "There is someone I think you need to meet," was all he said.

Bert called from the conference and told me what had happened and that he had invited Ted over for dinner the following week. He said, "He is bringing along a friend of his as well," he said. "She is from England. I hope that is all right with you?"

At the time, things were not going well for us personally. We were both very unhappy. Sooner or later something was going to give. It was either going to be our marriage or bankruptcy, or both. Entertaining at the time didn't have me all giddy with anticipation, to put it mildly. I wasn't much of a cook, and I considered myself to be a poor hostess. With a little encouragement from my husband and much hesitation on my part, I reluctantly agreed. As the evening progressed, however, it turned out that dinner was the last thing I needed to be concerned about.

When Ted arrived at our home, he introduced us to his friend, Sheila. After introductions were over, Sheila stepped forward into the hallway, dropped her arms down to her sides, and closed her eyes. Her behavior was totally unexpected and it caught us off guard. We stood there in stunned silence and looked at her, not sure if we were supposed to do anything or just wait. Ted smiled at us with this look of benevolent understanding and acceptance. Within a few seconds her arms began to move in and out from her sides in a very subtle manner.

Who is this woman? I thought to myself.

Ted continued to wait in respectful silence. Fascinated by her unusual behavior, we joined him in quiet respect, waiting for her to open her eyes again. Intuitively I could tell that she was checking out the energy in our home, but I didn't understand why it was necessary. But whatever she was doing, it felt important, so I said nothing. After about a minute, she opened her eyes and smiled at us.

That was different, I thought.

Sheila then asked if we would be so kind as to take her on a tour of our home. We found her request peculiar and a little intrusive, but quite frankly, by this point we were so intrigued with what she was up to that we would have pretty much agreed to anything. We dutifully took them both on a tour of the entire house.

We all walked through the entire house, with Sheila examining every single room, including the utility room. We were all very quiet during the tour, respecting Sheila's continued silence. After the "inspection" was over, we all sat down to dinner.

Ted was always fun to be with. He was never short of hilarious stories to share from his many adventures travelling around the world. Sheila, on the other hand, said very little the entire evening. After dinner was over and we were lingering over coffee and dessert, Sheila finally spoke up and asked if we would like to know why she wanted a tour of the house. She said, "Your home is not healthy. As a gift to you and in respect for having me over for dinner, I would like to offer suggestions on how to make your home a healthier one," she said. "Would you like to know what I have found?" she asked.

Personally, I was dying of curiosity. I looked over to my husband, who had this skeptical look on his face. We naturally both agreed to her analysis. For the next twenty minutes, Sheila proceeded to describe things to us about our lives that were very personal. She explained to us that we would never succeed financially and would continue to struggle with our health and happiness if we didn't make some changes. Quite frankly, we were both completely gobsmacked. We had never discussed our personal problems with Ted in the past, so there was no way he could have known we were struggling financially. That meant she couldn't have possibly known either. No one knew we were almost on the verge of declaring bankruptcy. Not even our families. I didn't know whether to laugh or cry. My husband sat in stunned silence. You could tell Ted knew this was coming. He sat there and grinned like a Cheshire cat.

I looked at her and said, "Okay, so how do we fix it?"

Sheila smiled at us sweetly and replied, "It is all very easily done." Sheila explained to us in minute detail what to do. I wrote it all down.

For the next six weeks, Bert and I were on a mission to make all the changes to our home that she had recommended.

The changes were simple and easy to do: paint, move a picture here or there, get some plants, fix a leaky tap, rearrange some furniture. One major suggestion she made was to change the way the front door opened. She suggested we hang it so that it opened in the other direction. We were in the process of looking for a new door anyway, so it was perfect timing. Within months of completing all the changes she recommended, our lives radically changed for the better. After ten years of pay cuts and part-time jobs, Bert got a new job, a raise, and a company car. I landed a full-time management contract. We learned about positive affirmations and how to use them. As a result, for the first time in years we had money in the bank, a new car, and jobs with benefits.

Sheila, it turned out, was a student of feng shui. We had never heard of it before, but she certainly had our undivided attention. That evening she explained some of the basic principles to us. Sheila taught us how important it was to manage the energy of a home. It was critical for health, happiness, and abundance. She told us that it should never be underestimated or ignored. We deeply appreciated all the advice she gave to us that evening. It was a valuable gift and a lesson that neither of us has ever forgotten.

Naturally, my interest was piqued about this thing called feng shui. I wanted to know more. I was on a mission, and I started to read every book I could get my hands on at the library. Eventually I took a course on feng shui and learned that the flow of energy through a home can dramatically affect a family's health, happiness, and sense of self-worth. At the course the instructor made an observation that really made a very deep impression on me. She said that everyone already intuitively practices the principles of feng shui—women in particular. A feeling of skepticism filtered around the classroom when she said that. Much to our surprise, she proceeded to prove it to each participant.

She asked each person to pick one room in their house and draw it out showing the placement of all major pieces in the room. After we were done, she walked around the room and explained to each participant how they had already intuitively placed things in the room for maximum harmony. For each layout, however, she would find one thing that was out of place and make a recommendation on where to move it. After she was done looking at everyone's layouts, she explained to us why each room had one thing out of place.

She told us that it was probably due to having mixed emotions about the piece because we either didn't like it, we were told we had to use it, we felt obligated to use it, or it was recommended by a well-meaning friend, relative, or partner. We all nodded in agreement. That was certainly true in my case. She went on to explain that if we paid attention to our instincts and arranged things the way that FELT right, we would change the energy of our homes without spending a lot of money or being concerned that we don't understand all the feng shui principles correctly.

Feng Shui and Energy Flow

Feng shui reminds us that everything in nature is made of energy. Whether it is something created in nature or by man, the life essence flows inside everything. Our homes are also energetic in nature. How they are organized significantly impacts how energy flows through the house and around the people living in the house. How a home is decorated and maintained is a direct reflection of whether the energy of the home is moving in a healthy way or if the energy becomes stuck. If the energy in a home is disrupted, it creates blockages. If there are enough blockages in place, the energy stops moving and everything in and around the home starts to get stuck. Cluttered space can make you feel anxious and stressed. The more clutter that is present, the more energy becomes stagnant. The more the energy can't flow through the home, the more indecisive you can become. It is a vicious circle. If your life is already complicated, clutter just adds an additional layer to your anxiety. Your sense of self-worth can plummet as a result.

All of this made sense to me. If the body is energetic in nature, then blockages in our aura could create problems physically, emotionally, mentally, or spiritually. It only stood to reason that our physical environment, where we lived and worked, could also be affected by blocked energy.

How do you know if your health and well-being is being hampered by the energy flow in your home? It's easier than you think. You will know if there is a problem if things seem to always go sideways around the house. Financial success is elusive. Your career never seems to get off the ground. You are always passed over for promotion. There is a constant stream of silly arguments with your partner over nothing. The kids always seem to wake up grumpy or bedtime behavior is impossible to manage. The house always looks like a tornado has just ripped through it. Family pets begin to have little accidents around the house, even though they are perfectly healthy. Electronics act up, light bulbs start to blow, the computer gets a virus, and light switches suddenly stop functioning. The mechanics of the house can start to act a little weird. The washing machine won't start, taps begin to leak, dishes get dropped—the list is endless. It can get very frustrating and annoying. Overall, everything feels off and out of balance somehow.

In *Creating Sacred Space with Feng Shui,* Karen Kingston writes "By adjusting and balancing the flow of energy within your home, you can powerfully and effectively influence the course of your life" (1996, 15).

It's crazy, but it can be that simple sometimes.

Sheila taught us how important it was to pay attention to how energy flowed through our home by paying attention to placement and color. The feng shui instructor taught me that paying attention to my intuition and giving myself permission to honor how I felt about the flow of energy through our house was also just as important. Doing both helped to make the dance much easier.

As a result of making the changes, we were moving with more ease through our lives. I started to realize that the more I paid attention to the flow of energy in my home, the more I learned that the flow wasn't just about placement and color, it was also about the emotional environment. The human body can get jammed up if things are not going well emotionally, just as the energy in a home can become stuck if the inhabitants are struggling with obstacles in their life. Both can contribute to stress and anxiety for the individual, while affecting how life flows for the entire family.

Space Clearing and Cleaning Up Energy Imprints

You don't have to be a student of feng shui to learn how to balance the energy in your home. You only need to give yourself permission to use your intuition and feel how things are moving in your home or space. Honor that inner wisdom that comes from your intuition. We all know that the way you dance depends on the music. We also know that music is sound energy that moves in waves that flow in a certain way. Everything we say or do also creates a sound that also moves in waves. Sound affects everything around it. Music can inspire you or make you cry. Your thoughts and feelings can make you happy or sad. Our eyes can see objects but we cannot see energy. We can feel it, though, and that is where intuition comes in.

Everything we say or do creates a vibration that ripples out and affects everything it touches. Like I have said earlier, two tuning forks in the same room will both begin to sing if only one tuning fork is tapped. Dr. Masaru Emoto states in his book *The Hidden Messages of Water* that, "The entire universe is in a state of vibration, and each thing generates its own frequency, which is unique" (2004, 39). He proved, through his research with water, that what we say to each other has a direct effect on the water content of our body. Since we are 70 percent water, it therefore affects the energy of our entire body. How we are resonating energetically does affect our surrounding environment. Most of us have had the unfortunate experience of working in a toxic environment. You can't prove it, but you can feel it. Working or living in a toxic environment can make you feel sick and directly impact your stress and anxiety levels.

High levels of negative emotions create toxic environments. The emotions sit in the air like a fog. We call these fogs "energetic imprints." Like a drink spilled on the dance floor, imprints stick to anything in a room, and it stays there until somebody cleans it up. You can't dance through life if you are getting stuck in what other people have left behind. If a deeply emotional or traumatic event happened in a room or home, then the energy is still present—unseen but intuitively felt. It hangs around like an unseen fog.

Imagine living in a home that never gets cleaned. After a while there is dust, dirt, cobwebs, and dust bunnies everywhere. You are afraid to sit down or touch anything because of the filth. It isn't healthy to live in a dirty house, and it isn't healthy to live in a house that is filled with toxic energetic imprints.

Physically clean houses can still be full of negative energetic imprints. Have you ever had the experience of entering a home and not feeling comfortable there? That's what happens when there are energetic imprints lingering in the room. The inner calm of your intuitive mind is making you aware that the room is full of stuck energy and that it isn't healthy.

The cool thing about understanding energy imprints and their vibrations is that you can change them from being negative into positive. Dr. Emoto proved that it was possible to change the energy of water using words, music, or intent, and he demonstrated those changes with pictures of frozen water.

Using the right combination of words and intents can easily cleanse a house of negative imprints. After the house is cleared, you can fill it energetically with any loving intent you choose. It is that easy.

When I first opened my practice as a medical intuitive, I worked out of my house. I was pretty busy, and I was seeing about 100 people a week for healing sessions. Because there were so many people coming and going from the house, it created a lot of movement in the energy of our home. As a result, I needed to balance the house weekly. After a while, I started to get out of the habit of clearing the house energetically. To be honest, I became lazy and complacent. Everything was going so well I didn't think I had to pay that much attention to it. That is until one day—out of the blue—all the lights and computers in the house flashed on and off again for about two minutes and then turned off. It was a regular little light show. The entire light show was a good reminder to me that when there is a lot going on, you need to pay attention to the energy imprints left behind.

One day I ran into a friend of mine who had recently won a beautiful new home that came fully furnished. As she was showing me the pictures of her new residence, which was really quite stunning, I asked her how she liked living there. I was surprised when she told me that in the beginning she and her husband had both hated living there and had a hard time settling in.

"That all changed, however, when I hired a colleague of yours to clear and balance the house energetically," she said.

As I looked at the pictures of the interior of house I could see why. I said, "It's no wonder. The house was filled with other people's energy."

She nodded in agreement and told me, "The house had been on display for over three months. We were told that over 5,000 people had toured through the home."

"Now that the house and land has been cleared and balanced, we love living there," she said with a big grin on her face.

Feng shui deals with the structure and function of how energy moves through a home. Space clearing deals with the energy imprints that fill the spaces in and around the objects of our home.

Clearing up the energy in your house is easy and quick. It doesn't need to be complicated, nor do you need to perform elaborate rituals. You can use a candle or incense if you like. Sage is always nice to use from time to time, but I would caution against using it before company arrives. Sage smells like marijuana and the neighbors can think something weird is going on. I know, because that is what happened to me after I cleared my house with sage on a summer day with all the windows open.

Preparing to Clear Space

Clearing your room or house is a powerful tool that can bring healing and joy back into your life. It is important to remember that as you prepare to clear your house, a few basic rules need to be followed. The space you are about to clear should be tidy and clean. You don't need to do a spring-cleaning, but dusting and vacuuming the space is highly recommended. If you wish to clear up a child's bedroom, that is wonderful, but if the child is a teenager, you will need their consent to clear their rooms. I often find that teenagers want to clear their room themselves, which I think is wonderful. I have seen teenagers not only clean their rooms but also repaint the walls after they have cleared their own space using this ceremony.

A Word about Intent

"Form follows thought" is an old, established esoteric teaching that clearly states, "What you think, you create." Everything is in motion. Everything is vibrating. Thoughts and feelings create vibrations. Space clearing uses this principle to create positive and powerful outcomes.

Your intent is very important and should be clear. What outcome are you hoping to achieve? What would you like to feel in the space? What feelings would you like your family to experience after the space clearing?

I like to write out my intent so I have a clear image of it in my mind before I begin.

At home the intent I set is: "To fill this house with love and light so all who enter here feel love, laughter, peace, joy, and safety."

In my waiting room and office, the intent I use is: "To fill this room with love and light so that all who enter here feel love, trust, and safety."

If I am having company over, I will use: "To fill this house with love and light so that all who enter here feel love, laughter, joy, and peace."

When I do space clearing, I like to use the power of angels to help clear the space. I work with the Archangels Michael, Gabriel, Raphael, and Ariel for the simple reason that these are the four angels I have always worked with. I like the fact that I can have one angel stand in each corner of a space or property to help shift and clear the energy. If you have four other angels that you prefer to work with, by all means feel free to change it up. I would recommend that you try to work with archangels though. They are a higher, purer form of spiritual consciousness.

Tools and Preparation

You should be well rested and well hydrated.

The room to be cleared should be clean and organized. Vacuum, dust, put away the toys and, clean up the clutter. Open the windows for a minute or two and allow fresh air into the room. Turn off the phone,

TV, computer, and stereo. Put the dog out or in another room. If you are clearing space in a bedroom, change the sheets on the bed, vacuum under the bed, and hang up all your clothes.

Wash your hands.

Have some incense and a lighter ready, and place them on a flame proof tray or dish. You can also substitute sage or a candle, if you prefer.

🪷 Exercise 🪷
Space Clearing—Room or Office

This ceremony should only take five or ten minutes.

1. Decide on the intent you wish to set before beginning. Write it down on a piece of paper.

2. Standing in the center of the room to be cleansed, take a few deep breaths and go into your Vertical Axis using the full procedure or your one word. (The Vertical Axis Technique, Step-by-Step, page 93)

3. As you light the incense, say out loud: *By the power invested in me by the Divine, I call upon the Archangels Michael, Gabriel, Raphael, and Ariel and ask you to be present with me in this room and to stand post in the four corners of this room.* Now imagine or pretend that you can see an angel standing in each corner of the room.

4. Holding the incense with one hand, say out loud: *I now ask the angels to clear this room of all negative and ungrounded energies at all levels, in all dimensions, in all time, and in all forms.*

5. Now walk around the room with the incense, and as you do so, use a sweeping motion of your hand to direct the smoke from the incense into the four corners of the room. When you are done, come back to the center of the room.

6. Now, picking up your written intent, return to the center of the room. Say out loud: *I ask the angels to please fill this room with divine love and light and protection.* Then read out loud the intent you have written down. Again, holding the burning incense,

walk around the room and use a sweeping motion with your free hand to direct the smoke into the four corners of the room. Pause here for a moment. Imagine that you can see or feel the room filling with a lovely white light or mist of love and light— this is carrying the energy of your intent into the room.

7. Place the incense back into a secure holder or flameproof dish. Place the dish in an area that is safe and won't be disturbed until it is finished burning. Thank the angels for their love, assistance, and guidance. Now imagine that they are smiling at you and sending you divine love and protection.

8. Say thank you or amen and see the angels leaving.

If you wish to use this procedure to clear your office, using incense probably won't be an option. Imagine or pretend you are using incense and walk around the room using your hand in a sweeping motion to move the energy out of the space. What is important here is that you are giving yourself permission to shift and move the energy in the space with your thoughts and intent.

❧ Exercise ❧
Clearing Space for House

This ceremony should only take fifteen to twenty minutes.

1. Decide on the intent you wish to set before beginning. Write it down on a piece of paper.

2. Standing in the center of the house to be cleansed, take a few deep breaths and go into your Vertical Axis.

3. As you light the incense, say out loud: *By the power invested in me by the Divine, I call upon the Archangels Michael, Gabriel, Raphael, and Ariel and ask you to be present with me in this house and to stand post at the four corners of this house.* Now imagine or pretend that you can see an angel standing in each one of the four corners of your house.

4. As you move around the house from room to room, holding onto the incense and with a sweeping motion of your hand, direct the smoke from the incense into the four corners of each room as you say: *I ask the angels to clear this room of all negative and ungrounded energies at all levels, in all dimensions, in all time, and in all forms.* Repeat this statement in each room. Be sure to walk through the entire house and clear all rooms in the house and garage.

5. When you are done, return to the center of your home. Now, picking up your intent, say out loud: *As I walk through this house, I ask the angels to please fill each and every room with divine love and light and protection.* Then read out loud the intent you have written down. Again, holding the burning incense, walk around each room in the house using a sweeping motion with your free hand to direct the smoke into the four corners of the room. Repeat the statement and your intent in each room. As you walk through the house, imagine that you can see or feel each room filling with a lovely white light or mist of love and light—this is carrying the energy of your intent into that room.

6. When you are done, return to the center of the house and place the incense back in a secure holder or flameproof dish. Place the dish in an area that is safe and won't be disturbed until it is finished burning. Thank the angels for their love, assistance, and guidance. Now imagine or pretend that they are smiling at you and sending you divine love and protection. Say thank you or amen and see the angels leaving.

🪷 Exercise 🪷
Clearing Space for Property

This ceremony should only take fifteen to twenty minutes.

When clearing your property, you have two options: You can perform the ceremony outside and walk around the property, or you can stand in the middle of your home and imagine or pretend that you are walking around the property. I prefer the latter. I live in a lovely community, but walking around my house or business with incense would create a public viewing. I prefer to keep it private.

1. Decide on the intent you wish to set before beginning. Write it down on a piece of paper.

2. Standing in the center of the house or property to be cleansed, take a few deep breaths and go into your Vertical Axis.

3. As you light the incense, say out loud: *By the power invested in me by the Divine, I call upon the Archangels Michael, Gabriel, Raphael, and Ariel and ask you to be present with me on this property and to stand post at the four corners of this property.* Now imagine or pretend that you can see an angel standing at each one of the four corners of your house or property.

4. Standing in the center of a room or the center of the house, visualize that you are moving around the property in your imagination. As you hold onto the incense, direct the smoke with a sweeping motion of your hand into the four corners of the property as you say: *I ask the angels to clear this property of all negative and ungrounded energies at all levels, in all dimensions, in all time, and in all forms.* Imagine that you are walking around the entire property clearing the space. Direct the smoke into all nooks and crannies of the property, including the outside of the house, any other buildings, the doghouse or chicken coup, if you have one.

5. When you are done, visualize returning to the center of your property. Pick up your intent, and say out loud: *As I walk around this property, I ask the angels to please fill all aspects of this property with divine love and light and protection"* Then read out loud the intent you have written down. Again, holding the burning incense, imagine you are walking around the property using a sweeping motion with your free hand to direct the smoke into the four corners of the property. As you walk around the property, imagine that you can see or feel the entire property filling with a lovely white light or mist of love and light—this is carrying the energy of your intent throughout the property.

6. When you are done, return to the center of the house and place the incense in a secure holder or flameproof dish. Place the dish in an area that is safe and won't be disturbed until it is finished burning.

7. Now ask the angels to surround your home and property with a Dome of Protection. Say out loud: *I ask the angels to surround my home and property with a dome of divine love and light so that all who live here are divinely loved, divinely guided, and divinely protected.*

8. Thank the angels for their love, assistance, and guidance. Now imagine or pretend that they are smiling at you and sending you divine love and protection. Say thank you or amen and see the angels leaving.

This ceremony can be used to balance cars, trucks, barns, stables, and office buildings. At my office the intent I set is: "All who enter here feel love, trust, and safety." Every day we hear from clients how much they love being at our Centre. They all say the same thing. "I feel safe here. The Centre is filled with love." All the practitioners who work here smile because they know that is the intent I have set for the property.

A Word About the Domes of Protection

A Dome of Protection is just that—a dome. It is energy with a set intent that covers the entire property. The domes can be set with different intents depending on the outcome you wish to achieve. When I moved my office out of my home and into a commercial office space, I wanted to make sure that my clients were directed to the new space. I used the Dome of Protection to make my house "disappear" to clients, and then I placed a different dome over my business so they could "find" our new location more easily. My clients had no trouble remembering our new location, but I was a little too effective on making my house "disappear." After I finished the ceremony to make my house disappear, I walked out of the house to go to our new business. At that very moment, a bird whizzed right by my head and slammed into the living room window.

The bird wasn't killed, thankfully, but I realized that I would have to go back inside and reset my intent with the house and energy dome. This time I asked that the energy dome cover the house in love and light and only able to be seen by all who lived in the neighborhood. This time when I stepped out of the house, another bird flew by, but this time he flew over the house. I thanked the angels for their quick reminder and for letting me know I had it right this time.

Clearing your energy field and your space reveals another level of just how powerful our thoughts and intentions can be. We can clear a lot of negative energy from our lives and our space. As you ponder the significance of this, it may leave you wondering about past events in your life that were painful. Maybe you will wonder, "If my thoughts are this powerful, what have I created in the past?" And that may have you asking, "Is there anything that can be done to heal the past?" Normally we are told you can't undo the past. Which, quite honestly, is true. But what if there was something that could be done to transform the energy that was created in the past so it doesn't affect your future?

13

Resolving Past Toxic
Relationships and Situations

Life happens and sometimes it can be pretty awful. After it's all over, you sit there battered and bruised and wonder how on earth did this happen. You find yourself wondering what to do next. Apologize? Forgive them for all the awful things they said to you? Blame God for making everything such a big mess? Or do you blame yourself for saying what was on your mind and try to find a way to live with the guilt? What if your actions made you feel shameful? How do you live with that? How do you hold your head up and keep moving forward? It can be the agony of the soul, living the human experience.

If you put enough emotional energy into the thought, then it creates an intent. Intents create a reaction and that reaction creates an effect or outcome. If you feed fear long enough and hard enough, it will create a reaction or response in your physical body. When you are angry, for example, your blood pressure will rise, your heart beats faster, and your breathing rate will change. Your skin becomes flushed with color and your body language changes. You become defensive, crossing your arms across your chest in an effort to protect yourself and anchoring your feet to stabilize your body. All this adrenalin pouring into your blood stream is making you feel afraid or threatened, just from a single thought.

On the other hand, when you feel love, your body softens. Your facial features relax and it is easy to smile and have a laugh. Your muscles relax. The warm glow you feel in your chest radiates out and everything in the world looks more vibrant, alive, joyful, and peaceful. All this from a single thought of love.

Fear is ego based. Love is based in the inner calm.

We are the architects of both, all with a single thought.

Life is nothing but a continual process of change.

In his book *Friendship with God: An Uncommon Dialogue*, Neale Donald Walsch reminds us that, "every act is an act of Self-definition. That is all you are doing here. You are defining and creating, expressing and experiencing, who you think you are. In short you are evolving. How you evolve is your choice. That you evolve is not" (1996, 373).

Whether an emotion is fear based or love based, it sets up a vibration in your aura that creates a change in your body's energy field. The vibration pulsates outwards into the world around you, like sound waves from a piece of music. That energy touches everything in your life. For women, it is the emotional subtext they pick up intuitively in every conversation. For men, it is the words that have been spoken along with the shift in body language that confirms what they are sensing intuitively. It is always there, seen or unseen, but present at a different level of intuitive awareness.

Everything in the universe responds to the same spiritual laws, one of which is called the Principle of Correspondence: "As above, so below; as below so above" (Initiates, 1912). Simplified, it means like attracts like. If you are feeling fear and speaking fear, you will attract more fear. If you are feeling love and speaking love, you will attract more love into your life. Remember the book and movie written by Rhonda Byrne called *The Secret*? Her book goes into great detail about how the law of attraction works in creating positive or negative experiences in our lives.

Remember, everything is energy—everything. Not only is your physical body energy, but every thought, feeling, and emotion you experience creates more energy. The scary part about this is that it means you are in control of what happens to you. The absolute best part about this is that it means you are in control of what happens to you. It is good and bad. Why? Because it reminds you that you have a choice on how life happens to you.

I remembered playing on the beach near our cottage when I was a child. My sister and I were lying down on a towel next to my mother. I was looking up at the clouds floating by in the sky. My mother asked us if we would like to learn how to dissolve clouds with our minds. As I said, Mother was never dull. She had us pick a tiny little cloud and imagine that we were sending a beam of light into the cloud and telling it to dissolve. Much to our excitement and glee, it worked! It was pretty cool. My mother told us, "That's the power of your mind."

The power of the mind.

The power of thoughts.

The vibrations that our thoughts create.

Dr. Emoto relayed an interesting story in his book, *The Hidden Messages of Water*. He tells the story of inviting a Shinto priest to repeat an incantation around the Fujiwara Dam in Japan to see what would happen to the quality of the polluted water. The entire ceremony took about an hour and was videotaped. About fifteen minutes after the priest had finished, someone noticed that the water was starting to clear. As they watched, the water became so clear they could see foliage at the bottom of the lake.

And I wondered.

Sometimes life goes a little sideways. We don't know why and we aren't always sure what part we had to play in the drama. However, it happened and now we are left with the aftermath of what to do next. Maybe a friend was upset and you misread the situation and failed to be loving enough in response. Maybe a relative is going through a tough period and you couldn't help at the time, or maybe you thought you were doing the right thing only to find out later that it was completely the wrong thing to do. Life happens. The bottom line is that the experience can be painful, gut-wrenching, and devastating. And it is really hard to come back from that and feel like you can stand up and love again. I know because I have been there too.

Relationships can go toxic at the drop of a hat. My mother developed a brain tumor. She became mentally ill, but we didn't realize what the problem was until it was too late. It happened so quickly and everything changed overnight. For a time, no one would believe me when I told them that something was terribly wrong with her. When I sought out medical help for her erratic and bizarre behavior, I was informed by the doctor that it was probably my fault and I needed to be on an antidepressant. I realized that I wasn't equipped to handle the situation properly. Her illness put me, personally, into emotional situations that I never would have dreamed of. She died six months later. After it was all over, I was angry for a long time. There was no room to grieve. There was only anger. It created problems in my relationships with the people I loved. The anger started to radiate outwards into other areas of my life. I found myself in ridiculous arguments that couldn't be resolved.

I needed to find a way to reverse all of this. It was infecting everything in my life and it had to stop. I understood that what was said and done was over. Everyone, including me, responded in the only way they knew how at the time. I understood I couldn't change the past but that didn't mean I couldn't find a way to let it go and move on. Sometimes it's just messy. And I wondered: if prayer could clear polluted water, what could prayer do to clear toxic energy that had been created around relationships?

I asked for divine guidance. I asked to be shown how to transform all the negative energy that was created by what was said and done into love and light so everyone could move forward and heal in love.

And this is what I was taught. I call them "Energetic Do-Overs."

Energetic Do-Overs

Over the years I have worked with this procedure, I have learned that it releases and removes the toxic energy created between two people and replaces it with love so that all parties involved can move forward. It sets up a more positive vibration so that the negativity doesn't multiply and cause more hurt. In most situations, I find that the conflict or upset fades away from memory. If any future discussion crops up around the matter, the situation doesn't seem to have the same level of emotional impact. In other situations it gave me the grace to walk away knowing that I did everything I could do and nothing was going to resolve the problem.

I have experienced great healing releases using this procedure. Not only has this procedure provided space for me to forgive myself, but it created space to forgive the "situation." In some situations the toxic relationship healed and developed into something more meaningful. In other situations the relationship came to an end and a deeper lesson was recognized. Energetic do-overs helped open the door to healing at a higher level of vibration. This technique is done privately. The other people involved need not be included nor informed. This technique is an instrument to assist you on your healing journey. It will help you to transform any negative energy created by you into a higher vibration of love and divine light. It neutralizes the fear transferred between two people and transforms it into love, which is a more powerful and positive healing vibration for both of you.

❧ Technique ❧
Energetic Do-Overs

This technique takes about ten to fifteen minutes. Have your journal and some pens ready to write down any thoughts or feelings you may have afterward.

1. Go into your Vertical Axis (page 93).
2. Imagine or pretend that you are standing in a sacred place. It can be a church, a field, a room, or a place in heaven.
3. Call in Archangel Michael (or a divine energy of your choice) and see him standing before you.
4. Call in the energy of the person you wish to create healing with.
5. Turn to Archangel Michael and say:
     I ask that anything I may have said, done, or thought about this person (state their name), that has been harmful or has al-

tered or blocked their life path in any way be transformed into
love and light for the good of all. I ask that all conflict between
us be healed with love in all directions and in all dimensions of
time. Amen

Then imagine you are looking into that person's eyes and say:

I love you. I am sorry. Please forgive me. Thank you.[5]

Then see yourself embracing that person. Release them and step back and see them being escorted by Archangel Michael back to their life. Stand in your place of love and gratitude for what they have taught you. See yourself coming back into awareness of where you are at this moment in time.

Energetic do-overs might not heal every toxic situation you find yourself in, nor will they necessarily create any miracles overnight. But it will release the negative vibration that toxic relationships can carry. Love is far more positive and healing than fear can ever be. Forgiveness for some people can be seen as a tricky thing, but it doesn't need to be.

Forgiveness

It can be really hard to forgive yourself and to forgive someone else. Forgiveness takes time. Some things are really too horrible to fathom. Other situations are just sad and so unnecessary. What's important is that you give yourself the space and mindset to begin the journey. In his book, *Disappearance of the Universe*, Gary Renard says that "forgiveness is unique, and designed to undo the ego—not by attack, but through the power of choice" (2002, 147).

I see this struggle for forgiveness in my practice all the time. When I am working with clients, we will discover blocks in their aura that hold a particular story. As we work through the story and question why it is there, I will ask if they have forgiven the person, and they will

---

5. A variation of the Ho'oponopona—an ancient Hawaiian practice of reconciliation and forgiveness.

often tell me they have. Yet I can tell from looking at their auras that what they said isn't true. Their auras will flash and swirl with seething anger and all manner of other emotions. When I ask them what is really going on with their forgiveness, the response is always the same. "I know I should forgive, so I have." Saying you *should* forgive someone when deep down you really haven't isn't very healing.

It is all right to be angry, hurt, upset, and resentful. We get angry and hurt when someone hasn't given us what we want. Your ego is expressing its judgments on the matter. Of course you are right and they are wrong. It is what the ego is all about. Pretending that something isn't the truth, as far as you are concerned, really only delays the inevitable. The wound will fester and find another outlet if you can't be honest with yourself.

I have found from experience that it is more productive to turn to the feelings and find out what your ego is really pissed off about. Write it down in your journal, go for a long walk, hit the pillow, but listen to what you are saying. Be the belly button. Read what you have written. You cannot change a mental thought pattern without looking at it first. Gandhi said we must be the change. This means WE have to be willing to change.

Have the courage to face your ego, turn into the problem, give yourself space to look at your beliefs and shift them, and release the toxic energy around it. With that choice comes the freedom to chart a new course for yourself. Forgiveness, as Debbie Ford says in her book, "needs to come from the heart, not the ego" (1998, 145). You can't get to the heart of the matter until you have faced what is blocking the love needed to heal.

I learned a long time ago that I could forgive the person, but that did not mean I had to condone the act. There is no excuse for bad behavior. But if I continued to allow my ego to constantly rehash the act in my mind, then I wasn't healing. The attack now had control over me. Turning inward to face the ego helped me stop that cycle of negativity. Listening to my intuition helped me review the story and then challenge it so I could process the fear, and this gave me the space I needed to find forgiveness.

Forgiveness is a process. Give it time. Let it come from the heart. You will know it when you get there. It feels different. If you are struggling with forgiveness, your connection to the inner divine can help you to shift your perspective if you ask it to. Forgiveness can be as simple as changing what you believe to be true. Don't let fear stop you from finding the freedom to discover that.

Conclusion:
Changing Your Dance for Good

What I love about dancing is that once you know the routine and have it committed to muscle memory, you have the freedom to go with the flow of the music. Being on the dance floor when everyone begins to move in an almost choreographed dance routine is magical.

Every dancer is a drop of water moving in harmony with the ocean of life. Everything is connected together in a unified dance. Your intuition is your teacher, showing you the right steps so that you can dance in harmony with the rhythm of life.

By discovering your dominant intuitive ability, you become more aware of how you are not your ego. It has no emotional context, only what it perceives to be the truth. This can be the lie that the ego thinks is the truth. Intuition, our connection to the inner divine, knows the truth. By allowing yourself to reconnect with the natural innate gift you were born with, you are finding your way back to the truth and living a life of truth, peace, love, and harmony. It helps us to overcome the root of our stress and anxiety, which is manufactured fear.

If you have already identified what type of intuitive you are, it is my hope that you are finding ways to practice it on a daily basis. It will teach you how to hear and understand the difference between ego's fear voice, which is manufactured fear, and intuition's calm, loving voice, which is your truth. This can dramatically reduce feelings of stress and anxiety because you can start to feel and identify the difference between the lies you think are truth and what the truth really is. You are becoming empowered.

Explore the different aspects of your soul development and separation from the Divine. Ask yourself if there were events in your life that hampered your soul separation. Are there any events that you can safely revisit to reassess how you want to change its beliefs? Journal your story. Find out where the ego is confused, reach out with the inner calm using your intuition, and help it shift its perspective.

As you develop your intuitive gifts, carry a copy of the intuitive ethics with you. It will be so much easier for you to understand how and when to use this gift. Remember, just because you think you know, doesn't mean you do. Temper what you intuitively know to be the truth and wait to be asked, and then only do as asked. Be honest in your responses. Learn to respect other people's choices and how they choose to accept what they asked for. If they refuse help, send them love. Honor their soul's journey. We may not always know why a loved one makes the choices that they do, but it is not our place to judge the journey they are undertaking. Always check in to see if what you are feeling or sensing is really yours. It can make everything you experience so much easier.

Be the belly button and explore your subconscious beliefs. Uncover the stories that make you afraid and embrace them. Use your intuition to be with the wounded inner child of your ego, and bring love and comfort there. Fear is just a very scared little child looking for love. Let your intuition be the adult in the room, teaching the ego how to embrace the goodness that exists there. Find the pattern, figure out what you are trying to learn, and embrace the wisdom. Be loving and kind to your own human journey.

Give yourself permission to sleep deeply and restfully. Let the angels help you find solutions to problems. Allow them to guide you in the dreamtime so your time there is more purposeful. Give your body the rest it needs to repair and restore physically, emotionally, and mentally. Record your dreams and let them reveal some of the mysteries of life that can be found there.

We are what we think. We manifest what we believe. We have a choice in what we believe and we have the will power to change our reality. The ego will attempt to undo what you are trying to manifest because it is afraid of change. This is doubt. The universe will try to speed up the process of helping you manifest what is more loving. That's the blip. Let the blips—the universal bulldozer—do their job of speeding up the process of a new belief system. Face the blip with a smile and keep on dancing to the new routine.

It is because we are so connected to each other that we react and form judgments based on what we feel. If a butterfly flapping its wings in North America can affect the weather in Africa, then your thoughts do resonate with the people you think about. To heal these energetic connections, you can utilize the power of angels to help you clear the energetic and emotional debris through cord cutting and space clearing. Like the power of prayer, you can clear space and heal relationships by freeing them of negative imprints and misplaced intents.

With the power of intent to create form, we can protect our auras in safe and loving ways without getting attached, attacked, or drained. Shields can be used when you want to be present but protected; cloaking when you want privacy; and the White Light of Protection when you feel vulnerable or need to deal with issues that could be potentially hurtful and upsetting.

With our power of intuition we can also begin to identify when we are being manipulated. With that recognition there comes a call to action to reaffirm our self-respect and honor our own needs. Learning how to say no and stand our ground in a loving way, despite what others may say, is sometimes tough. But it is necessary if one wishes to be free from any form of emotional manipulation and walk away from toxic relationships that have no purpose other than to serve and create fear. These are the gifts our intuition can give us—that inner reassurance that what the other is saying is untrue. We should never be afraid to acknowledge that our truth may not be the same as another person's truth.

Then there is the power of forgiveness—releasing ourselves of negative intent so we can not only be free, but we can also free our loved ones of the energy we created out of our misplaced fear, anger, and judgments.

Where do you begin the intuitive dance so you can stop battling your ego and find your inner calm? Begin with the Three Simple Things located in the Appendix on page 225. For a total of five minutes a day, you can ground using the Vertical Axis in the morning, cut fear cords with the angels in the evening, and manage your dreamtime at bedtime.

Being in the Vertical Axis will help you clear the mental chatter, calm the mind, manage your fear, help you to make decisions more easily, and allow you to access the inner calm more easily. You will have a deeper sense of empowerment, and you will be less likely to be manipulated by other people's personal agendas.

Doing the cord cutting in the evening frees you of the static that you have picked up from everyone you have been in contact with throughout the day, including the people you love. Remember the fear cord cutting technique will not and cannot cut love cords.

Finish with the dreamtime management. This will help guide you to the right place in the astral plane so you can receive a deep restorative sleep.

Try doing the self-directed survey for forty days and tracking your progress to feeling calmer, sleeping better, and feeling more peaceful.

Next I would suggest doing the quiz to find your dominant intuitive skill, if you haven't already.

Once you have identified your dominant intuitive ability, practice using it daily. Journal what you pick up intuitively and what you think you missed. Review your notes to discover just how much you were probably picking up. Don't be afraid to use different colored pens with your journaling. Find a color pen for your voice, one for your ego rants, and another for what you think are your intuitive impressions.

As you become more comfortable with your intuitive abilities and you feel more grounded, more rested, and less reactive, try shielding. Acknowledge how it helps you manage the amount you feel and when you feel it as you go through your day. If you need more privacy, try putting on your cloak. Practice using your cloak in public and see how much more comfortable you feel in public places. See if you are less overwhelmed and confused when you are at the mall or grocery store. If you feel you are going to be in a very emotionally charged situation, use the White Light of Protection.

Don't forget to find out what your one word is for the Vertical Axis and your shields and cloaks of protection. You never know when you are going to need them, and it is nice to know you have the power to call on them at a moment's notice.

Next I would begin to play with space clearing. Try it at home, and then try it at your office. See if things change. Record your observations in your journal. Practice using different types of domes over your home and see what happens.

Listen to how much calmer your ego voice is becoming. Do you notice that there are times during the day when your mind is silent? You may notice that there are times during the day when you feel waves of love surrounding you and you feel at total peace. If they happen, pause, be with them, and breathe. Once they begin, they will reoccur on a regular basis.

Begin to observe how you are interacting with others. Are you able to recognize when they are making efforts to manipulate you into following their agendas? Are you noticing when you encounter an energy tyrant or an emotional blackmailer? What does your intuition tell you? What guidance are you receiving from your intuition to help you cope?

The battle between your ego and intuition is one of separation versus connection. It is the classic battle of fear versus love. This battle is the conflict that creates anxiety because you don't know who to believe. Your ego comes from a place of fear. Fear is tangible, visceral, cold, physical, and exclusive. Intuition comes from a place of love. Love is more elusive, ethereal, warm, and inclusive. Trying to describe what love feels like is almost impossible, isn't it? How I feel and express love isn't going to be the way you experience it. Is your reality of love right or is my reality of love right? What if we are both right? What if it is all right for each to have a different experience? When did your reality become right and mine become wrong? It never did, but our egos will try to convince us of that. That is separation. Our intuition is trying to show us that it is all right to be different, because at our core we are all the same. We are all connected. We are each having an individual experience. It is the soul having a human experience.

My acceptance of how I love and your acceptance of how you love is connection. It is how we allow our human experience to find its way back to the soul. If you honor your experience as your truth and you honor my experience as my truth, we are both in a place of love acceptance without ego attachment. Mutually respecting and honoring our free will is unity, compassion, and empathy. One moment we feel love and we belong. Life feels beautiful, inclusive. The next minute we might feel afraid, separate, misunderstood, all from a single thought or a conclusion. It is hard to find "proof" of a thought or feeling. The ego is always thinking and connecting to the visceral experience. Our intuition is always feeling the love and connection to the Divine. The more you learn to listen and follow your natural intuitive ability, the easier it will become to feel the love connection, despite what the ego experience is. It is giving yourself permission to be continually aware of that energy of love and peace, even in the midst of a physical experience that is fearful, confusing, or uncomfortable. It is being grounded into both the physical and ethereal experience at the same time and being in control of how you choose to experience it.

As you embrace your intuition, you realize that you are no longer just a drop of water. Let yourself embrace the magic of being in the ocean and explore how interconnected you really are. You may not be able to change the world, but by shifting your awareness, you become the change. Imagine the possibilities if we all woke up to our innate inner wisdom.

We all want to lead peaceful, loving, and productive lives. It is hard to accept that so much of the stress and anxiety we experience in life is the result of our own manufactured negativity. Yet, when we realize that so much of this inner turmoil is of our own making, and we understand the power of choice and free will, the journey doesn't seem to feel so tedious. We have been shown a way out of a mental quagmire by using our intuition to guide us back to the inner calm, which is offered to us by the Divine. There are only two emotions, love and fear. We have the right of choice. Embrace it. Dance with it. Be the intuitive who dances with life and stop battling your ego and be with your inner calm. It is a gift from the Divine.

Appendix:
A 40-Day Practice
Using Three Simple Things

When you are stressed out, freaked out, or you feel like your life is falling to pieces, the last thing you want to hear from anybody is maybe you should read a book to help you find a way to cope. Over the course of working with clients who were in similar situations, I started to give them three simple energetic exercises that only took a total of five minutes a day to complete. The feedback I received from them was quite surprising. Everyone said that it actually made a lot of difference in how they were able to cope with their stress and anxiety. I started to wonder if we could actually measure the effectiveness of these techniques.

A colleague of mine, Roxana Roshon, PhD, a research scientist and holistic healer, was visiting one day and I asked her if she thought there was a way we could measure the impact that the Three Simple Things were having on reducing stress and anxiety. "Absolutely," she said. Together with a mutual colleague, Michelle Cali, ND, we crafted a study for thirty volunteers to do the Three Simple Things for five minutes a day over a forty-day period.

The results were amazing. The research proved that by doing the Three Simple Things, there was a 10 to 50 percent improvement in how participants handled stress and anxiety. They felt calmer and more peaceful, and they found that they had more clarity about their sense of direction and purpose in life. Volunteers reported that they couldn't believe that doing the Three Simple Things could make such an improvement in their quality of life.

What are the three things?

1. The Vertical Axis (The Vertical Axis Technique, Step-by-Step, page 93)
2. Cord cutting with the Angels (Fear Cord Cutting Technique, page 183)
3. Dreamtime Management (Dreamtime Management Technique, page 111)

As discussed earlier in the book, anxiety is defined as a nervous disorder marked by excessive uneasiness and apprehension, typically with compulsive behavior or panic attacks. Stress is defined as a state of mental or emotional strain that results from adverse or demanding circumstances.

As we can see from these definitions, anxiety and stress are due to underlying emotions of uneasiness and apprehension. This is where the ego excels. It creates a constant emotional environment of self-doubt and inner criticism in the subconscious that challenges every thought and action we have. Much of what we are taught about how to manage stress and anxiety is through diet, exercise, and rest. All of these techniques are useful, I agree, and they do help to alleviate the physical toll of stress and anxiety on our bodies, yet it doesn't address the emotional undercurrent. How we feel and think about what is happening to us is created by our ego. Our ego analyzes and responds to emotional and physical stresses, which often results in escalating fear reactions to what is happening in our lives. Doesn't it stand to reason that if you address the emotional undercurrent of ego-driven thought patterns, it would be much easier to handle the physical environment under duress? Doesn't it stand to reason that the emotional mind drama can be managed and channeled to help us cope with life in a more loving and grounded way?

Through our research we were able to prove that doing the Three Simple Things could help people take control of their ego's emotional reactions to events while developing more appropriate strategy's to managing their stress and anxiety. Volunteers reported that they slept better, improved their diets, and were able to identify when they were reacting to other people's emotions. They felt more relaxed, happier, and content. The Three Simple Things helped them manage their ego and dance with their intuition

40-Day Study

During the forty-day period, volunteers were asked to do the Three Simple Things each day. Volunteers were also asked to complete a survey at three periods during the forty-day study. We then measured and calculated the results. At the end of the study, the relative percent difference for each participant was calculated for each question. Questions were randomly mixed between the three surveys. Questions were either yes or no or they were ranked on a scale of 1 to 10, depending on the type of question.

Results for Questions ranked on a scale of 1 to 10

Question	% Change
Has there been a decrease in how much you worry about others?	15% improvement
Have you noticed a decrease in the need to please others?	11.5% improvement
Have you noticed a decrease in the level of worry?	18.2% improvement
Have you noticed an increase in energy?	17.1% improvement
Is it easier to fall asleep?	13.1% improvement
Has there been a change in your level of worry when you try to sleep at night?	27.8% improvement

Results for Yes or No Questions:

Question	% Change
Are you a worrier?	13.8% improvement
Is it hard to fall asleep?	31% improvement
Are you easily influenced by others?	41.4% improvement
Do you worry a lot at night when you are going to bed?	34.5% improvement
Have you noticed any other changes?	55.2% improvement

Comments noted in the final survey

In addition to the yes or no questions, which showed the most dramatic shift for volunteers, almost all of the volunteers reported verbally to the researchers how much they felt the study helped them over the forty-day period. They were very enthusiastic about the Three Simple Things and had every intention of continuing with the exercises now that the study was complete.

Overall we found that:

- The volunteers felt calmer and more conscious
- The study made the majority of volunteers re-examine different aspects of their lives more closely

Written Comments from the Survey

- "I am grateful to Atherton for this study. I now have a great tool to manage my daily stresses."
- "The Vertical Axis has now become a healthy habit and has propelled me to begin studying Reiki."
- "The Vertical Axis is a powerful tool for peace and goodwill."
- "The Vertical Axis taught me how to meditate and it decreased my stress levels and made my life calm."
- "I will continue to use the tools provided to me as part of this study. I feel an increase in my overall purpose and satisfaction and security in life. I enjoyed the inner peace and contentment I feel."

• "Enhanced sense that I can be in control if needed. Provided me with security knowing that I have an effective tool that significantly helps me to feel better."

• "I feel much lighter, brighter, and happier. I find it easier to cope with life. My dreams are very rich and informative. I am more at peace and am able to release people with ease."

• "Mental chatter at night is all gone! Therefore feel more rested and have noticed a difference in my ability to focus on tasks at hand. After two years I have finally been able to resolve conflicts around my mother's estate and feel motivated to deal with her belongings."

What are these three simple steps?

1. The most dynamic grounding technique you will ever learn—The Vertical Axis

2. Cutting energy cords with everyone you have been in touch with on a daily basis using the power of angels

3. Create deep restorative sleep almost immediately by practicing a simple technique called Dreamtime Management

These three quick and simple steps, when practiced daily for just a few minutes each day, could very well change your life almost immediately. I know, because I have taught them to hundreds of clients for the past fifteen years, and they work!

If you would like to see how the Three Simple Things exercise can help you handle stress and anxiety in your life, and give you a greater sense of control and peace, this is what you can do.

Three Simple Things

For the next forty days, you are agreeing to do three things each day.

All these exercises combined should not take more than 5 minutes a day. If it is taking longer than that, then you are trying too hard. Relax, breathe, and have some fun with it. If you can't see it or feel it, not to worry. It is still there. It's all right to imagine that it is happening. In energy medicine, form always follows thought. Therefore if you are thinking it, you are creating it.

Each Morning
Vertical Axis

Each Evening
Vertical Axis, Cord cutting, Dreamtime Management

The Vertical Axis Technique
Refer to the Vertical Axis Technique, Step-by-Step, page 93.

You can receive a free download of the Vertical Axis if you sign up for the free newsletter, "The Paradigm Pages," at *www.athertondrenth.ca*, where a full audio version of the Vertical Axis is also available for sale.

Cord Cutting with the Angels
Refer to Fear Cord Cutting Technique on page 183.

Dreamtime Management with the Angels
Refer to the Dreamtime Management Technique on page 111.

Monitor your success
If you would like to monitor your success in handling stress and anxiety complete the following survey at the beginning, middle and end of the forty-day period. As we know from other research,[6] it takes forty days to reprogram our minds to change a habit. Make the Three Simple Things part of your healthy self-care plan.

If you are currently experiencing some dramatic life changes, you may find that doing the Three Simple Things can help you to stay grounded, get some much needed rest, and have a stronger ability to cope.

---

6. John Randolph Price's *The Abundance Book* cites the effectiveness of chanting a belief system over a forty-day period.

Survey

On a scale of 1 to 10, where 1 is low/easy/not at all and 10 is high/difficult/frequently:

How much do you worry about what other people think of you?

1   2   3   4   5   6   7   8   9   10

How important is it for you to please others?

1   2   3   4   5   6   7   8   9   10

How would you rate your level of worry?

1   2   3   4   5   6   7   8   9   10

How would you rate your current level of exhaustion?

1   2   3   4   5   6   7   8   9   10

How much would you say you worry at night when you are falling asleep?

1   2   3   4   5   6   7   8   9   10

How hard is it to fall asleep at night?

1   2   3   4   5   6   7   8   9   10

Are you a worrier?

Yes   No

Is it hard to fall asleep?

Yes   No

Do you feel that you are easily influenced by other people's opinions?

Yes   No

Do you worry a lot at night when you go to bed?

Yes   No

Have you noticed any other changes?

Yes   No

If yes, describe what changes you have noticed.

_____

_____

_____

_____

Worksheet to Record Your Results

On a scale of 1 to 10, where 1 is low/easy/not at all and 10 is high/difficult/frequently

Question	Day One	Day Twenty	Day Forty
How much do you worry about what other people think of you?			
How important is it for you to please others?			
How would you rate your level of worry?			
How would you rate your current level of exhaustion?			
How much would you say you worry at night when you are falling asleep?			
How hard is it to fall asleep at night?			

Watch Your Numbers Drop

If your answers have decreased in value, then you are experiencing improvement in how you deal with the emotions that make stress and anxiety a challenge in your life.

Answers to yes or no questions. If you are unsure, record M for maybe.

Question	Day One	Day Twenty	Day Forty
Are you a worrier?			
Is it hard to fall asleep?			
Do you feel that you are easily influenced by other people's opinions?			
Do you worry a lot at night when you go to bed?			

If your answers have gone from yes to no, then you are experiencing significant improvement in how you deal with the emotions that make stress and anxiety a challenge in your life.

The Three Simple Things research study was developed, administered, and compiled by: Atherton Drenth, medical intuitive, Roxana Roshon, PhD, and Dr. Michelle Cali, ND.

Glossary

affirmations: Statements of belief that are aimed at influencing and directing the conscious and subconscious mind to create change mentally, emotionally, and spiritually in a person's life. These statements activate a spiritual principle called the law of attraction.

angels: Beings of divine light who act as messengers between God or the divine forces of the universe that have been created here on earth. They are considered to be servants of God and guardians of all life on earth and are often referred to in many religious texts and teachings.

anxiety: A nervous disorder characterized by a state of excessive uneasiness, such as a constant concern about imminent danger or difficulties that may or may not occur.

archangels: Angels of high rank that oversee and manage angels and other guardians in the lower hierarchies of heaven. They are frequently depicted in religious teachings as beings of light who bring messages directly from God.

astral body: Also called the "ether body." It is the subtle energy field that is seen by clairvoyants as a kind of double of the physical body. It is holographic in nature and can be seen or felt using one's intuitive abilities or viewed using the third eye.

astral plane: A bridge between the spiritual and physical bodies. It is a real place and is holographic in nature.

aura: An electromagnetic field around all living things. Human beings have the most complex energy field and it is comprised of four major layers: physical, emotional, mental and spiritual. These four levels are also referred to as "subtle bodies." It is perceived as a light or luminous body that moves around the physical body. It can be seen or felt using one's intuitive abilities.

auric field: Surrounds the human body and links it with the chakra energy bodies. It is egg shaped and projects out from the physical body from ten to twenty feet, depending on the life force of the body.

awakening: Becoming conscious of the spiritual side of life. As one becomes more conscious, they are aware of their impact on the world around them either through physical, emotional, mental, or spiritual beliefs and actions. It is also referred to as becoming aware of "being one with the All."

Buddha: Born as Siddhartha Gautama in Nepal around 2,500 years ago. He did not claim to be a god or a prophet. He was a human being who became enlightened—understanding life in the deepest way possible.

Buddha is a also title, which means "one who is awake" in the sense of having woken up to reality.

Chakra: The Sanskrit word for wheel, signifying one of seven basic energy centers in the body. Each of these centers correlate to major nerve ganglia branching out from the spinal column, and they are related to various specific physical and emotional components.

Christ light: Also called universal healing light, spirit light, God light, Divine love, healing light, etc. In healing work, there is a rule that when something is removed energetically from the body's energy field, a vacuum cannot be left behind. This vacuum is always filled with divine healing light and speeds up body healing. Healers are trained specifically to do this in a grounded, heart centered, and loving way to assist with the body's healing.

clairaudience: Clear hearing that utilizes one's ability to receive intuitive guidance inside the mind. The information can be received as statements, sounds, songs or lyrics. It is sensed as a vibration and received in the clairaudient center, located just above the ears in the temporal lobe area.

claircognizance: Clear knowing that utilizes one's ability to receive intuitive guidance as a hunch or an impression. Claircognizants have two areas where information can be received: either through the top of the head—the crown chakra—or through the heart—the fourth chakra.

clairsentience: Clear feeling that utilizes one's ability to receive information or guidance physically anywhere in the body. It is also called having a body clue. The clairsentient center is located in the middle of the belly or solar plexus, which is also called the third chakra.

clairvoyance: Clear seeing that utilizes one's intuitive ability to see things inside the mind as pictures, images, short movies, symbols, or impressions. The clairvoyant center is located in the third eye, which is also called the sixth chakra.

crown chakra: See seventh chakra.

ego: That part of the mind that has a sense of individuality and is most conscious of self. It deals with external reality.

electroencephalograms (EEG): A test that measures and records the electrical activity of the brain. This procedure is used to determine if the brain is functioning properly.

energy field: Also referred to as an aura or human energy field. It is a set of energy bands that graduate in frequency and color as they move away from the body. It is also connected to the chakra system.

energy therapy: A type of healing technique that acts as an interpreter for the body's innate wisdom. Energy therapy can be practiced by energy workers, energy medicine practitioners, medical intuitives, and healers.

energy worker: Also called a healer or energy medicine practitioner. They practice the healing arts and act as interpreters for the body's innate wisdom.

etheric body: An energetic template or blueprint for the physical body. It lies just above the physical body and is said to provide health, vitality, and organization to the physical body. It is usually the first to be seen when one's intuitive ability to see auras manifests. It is also referred to as the template for our physical body. The etheric body connects us to our higher energy bodies.

fear cords: Energetic representations of fear either produced or received from another person. They appear as cords coming out of the body and can vary in texture, color, size, depth, thickness, and emotional nature. They are most commonly found between parents and their children, but they can also be found from other people if there has been a strong emotional connection between the two. Fear cords are very easy to remove either by the client themselves or with assistance from a healer.

feng shui: An ancient oriental philosophy of harmonizing people with their environment by balancing the flow of energy (qi).

fifth chakra: Also called the throat chakra. It represents how we communicate with the world. It is situated over the throat.

first chakra: Also called the root chakra. It represents how we stand in the world. It is found at the base of the tailbone.

fourth chakra: Also called the heart chakra. It represents love. It is located in the center of the chest.

gas distribution visualization (GDV): A technique using a special type of camera to record images of an aura for analysis.

hara: Located three fingers below the navel, it is considered to be the center where everything that we are is balanced, physically and energetically. It is also believed to be the point in which the silver cord of life enters into the body.

heart chakra: See fourth chakra.

hologram: A photographic technique that records light emitted from an object and then displays it in a way that appears to be three-dimensional.

intuition: The power of understanding situations or people's feelings immediately, without the need for conscious reasoning or study. It is believed to be connected to the Divine source of consciousness.

Jesus Christ: The central figure of modern Christianity, considered to be the savior for all mankind.

Kirlian Photography: A special form of photography used to take pictures of auras by using high-frequency electrical pulses while recording it on film.

kundalini: A term used to describe the feminine life energy as it rises up through the spine to meet its complementary male energy. Different spiritual traditions teach their own methods of "awakening" kundalini for reaching enlightenment. Some traditions describe the kundalini as lying coiled at the base of the spine like a sleeping serpent or goddess waiting to be woken.

law of attraction: A belief system taught by ancient mystics that explains one of the most powerful laws that govern the universe. The law of attraction states: As is above, so it is below. This means that what we think, we create, and what we create, we think.

meditation: Considered to be an exercise for the mind to assist in deeper contemplation and self-reflection. Regular meditation helps one learn how to transform and manage the mind and thought activity in order to enhance one's ability to concentrate and cultivate a deeper understanding of human nature and the nature of life.

mental body: An energetic layer of the aura that holds our mental thoughts even after the event has occurred. It holds our ideas, thoughts, and beliefs about who we are in the world.

Mother Mary: Considered to be the mother of Jesus Christ who is said to have conceived him through the Holy Spirit. She is also considered to be a saint by various religions.

movies: A term used in energy work to refer to an event that will occur in healing sessions. The energy body records all events that happen to the body. It will replay the event as it happened in order to explain why the body is holding pain or trauma. They are short, visual, and seen through the third eye. They can be symbolic of what the body is trying to say or they can be an actual replay of a memory. Movies are relayed to the client by the healer and then the client determines whether they feel right or true for them.

muscle memory: A form of memory that occurs when the same action is repeated over and over again. The mind no longer has to think about the action. Movement is automatically repeated in a known pattern. Dancing, walking, jumping, or talking are all considered to be forms of muscle memory.

mystic: One who has intimate, firsthand acquaintance with God; a man or woman of prayer. Jesus was one of the greatest mystics of all time. All saints and great spiritual teachers are considered to be mystics, such as Buddha and Muhammad.

nadi: An energy channel connected to the hara. It directs the vital life energy from the hara out into our chakra system. This system is the energetic nervous system of our energetic body or aura.

Noble Truths: The Four Noble Truths make up the essence of Buddha's teachings. They are the truth of suffering, the truth of the cause of suffering, the truth of the end of suffering, and the truth of the path that leads to the end of suffering.

pineal gland: A pea-sized conical mass of tissue found in the middle of the brain.

rapid eye movement : Known as REM sleep, one of the five stages of sleep that most people experience nightly. It is characterized by quick random movements of the eyes and paralysis of the muscles.

root chakra: See first chakra.

second chakra: Also called the sexual chakra. It represents how we express our sexuality and creativity. It lies midway between the pubic bone and belly button.

seventh chakra: Also called the crown chakra. It represents our connection to the Divine and our spirituality. It is situated at the top of head.

sexual chakra: See second chakra.

sixth chakra: Also called the third eye. It represents intuition and what we see of the world. It is situated in the middle of the forehead, above the eyes.

solar plexus: See third chakra.

soul: The spiritual or immaterial component of a human being or animal, regarded as the seat of the emotions or intellect. The soul is also considered to act as a link between the physical body and the spiritual or higher self. In some religions it is believed to be a spark of the divine or God that exists within the body.

spiritual body: An energetic layer of the aura that is our connection to the Divine. It is the outermost layer of the aura and holds our spiritual beliefs.

stress: A condition or adverse circumstance that disturbs or is likely to disturb the normal physiological or psychological functions of an individual.

subtle bodies: The aura is comprised of seven layers known as the subtle bodies. Each layer holds different information and is connected to the chakras. The subtle bodies expand and contract accordingly, depending on the information or thoughts that the body is experiencing at that moment in time.

Sufi: A Muslim ascetic and mystic who is a devout follower of God. Sufi's teach that one should remember God and be of service to others.

Theosophy: A system of belief based on mystical insight into the nature of God and the soul. It holds the belief that all religions are attempts by the spiritual hierarchy (Ascended masters and spiritual teachers such as Saint Germain or Lord Maitreya, etc.) to help humanity in evolving to greater perfection; therefore each religion has a portion of the truth.

third chakra: Also called the solar plexus. It is the chakra of self-esteem and represents how safe it is to express ourselves in the world. It lies between the belly button and the rib cage.

third eye: An etheric organ of intuitive (psychic) perception that sees beyond the physical world. It is located in the middle of the forehead and is associated with the "brow" or sixth chakra. It is believed to be associated with the pineal gland.

throat chakra: See fifth chakra.

Zen: A form of Buddhism emphasizing the value of meditation and intuition. Being Zen means that one has the characteristics thought to be typical of tranquility and peaceful acceptance.

Bibliography

Alexander, Eben, MD. *Proof of Heaven: A Neurosurgeon's Journey into the Afterlife.* New York: Simon & Schuster, 2012.

Bach, Richard. *Illusions: The Adventures of a Reluctant Messiah.* New York: Random House, 2012.

Brennan, Barbara Ann. *Light Emerging: The Journey of Personal Healing.* New York: Bantam Books, 1993.

Byrne, Rhonda. *The Secret.* New York: Atria Books, 2006.

Dale, Cyndi. *The Subtle Body: An Encyclopedia of Your Energetic Anatomy.* Boulder, Colorado: Sounds True, 2009.

Dass, Ram. *Journey of Awakening: A Meditator's Guidebook.* New York: Bantam Books, 1990.

Dispenza, Joe. *Evolve your Brain: The Science of Changing Your Mind.* Dearfield, FL: Health Communications, 2007.

Emoto, Dr. Masaru. *The Hidden Messages in Water.* Hillsboro, OR: Beyond Words Pub., 2004.

Ford, Debbie. *The Dark Side of the Light Chasers: Reclaiming Your Power, Creativity, Brilliance, and Dreams.* New York: Riverhead Books, 1998.

Hay, Louise. *I Can Do It: How to Use Affirmations to Change Your Life.* Carlsbad, CA: Hay House, 2004.

Initiates, The Three. *The Kybalion: The Seven Ancient Principles.* Chicago: Yogi Publication Society, 1912.

"Intuition." *Oxford Dictionaries.* Oxford University Press, accessed May 26, 2016, http://www.oxforddictionaries.com/us/definition/american_english/intuition

Kingston, Karen. *Creating Sacred Space with Feng Shui.* London: Piatkus, 1996.

Leadbeater, C. W. *Astral Plane: Its Scenery, Inhabitants and Phenomena* (1898). Facsimile of the first addition. Montana: Kessinger Publishing, 1996.

Lipton, Bruce H., PhD. *The Biology of Belief: Unleashing the Power of Consciousness, Matter & Miracles.* Carlsbad, CA: Hay House, 2008.

Mathieson, Andrea. "The Raven Essence Manual: A Love Affair with Nature." Maple, Ontario: Raven Essences, 2003.

Morley, Charlie. *Dreams of Awakening: Lucid Dreaming and Mindfulness of Dream and Sleep.* London: Hay House, 2013.

Price, John Randolph. *The Angels Within Us.* New York: Fawcett Columbine, 1993.

Renard, Gary R. *The Disappearance of the Universe.* Carlsbad, CA: Hay House, 2004.

Sanders, Pete A. Jr. *You are Psychic: The Free Soul Method.* New York: Fireside, 1989

Sharp, Jonathan. *Divining Your Dreams.* New York: Simon & Schuster, 2002.

Sherwood, Keith. *Chakra Therapy: For Personal Growth and Healing.* St. Paul, MN: Llewellyn Publications, 2002.

"Sleep and Dream: Disorders," Dr. W. Dement and Dr. E. Jones. Accessed Oct. 28, 2015, https://sites.google.com/site/sleepanddreamsdisorders/home.

Tolle, Eckhart. *A New Earth: Awakening to Your Life's Purpose.* New York: Penguin Books, 2006.

Walsch, Neale Donald. *Conversations with God: An Uncommon Dialogue, Book 1.* New York: G. P. Putnam's Sons, 1996.

Index

To Write to the Author

If you wish to contact the author or would like more information about this book, please write to the author in care of Llewellyn Worldwide Ltd. and we will forward your request. Both the author and publisher appreciate hearing from you and learning of your enjoyment of this book and how it has helped you. Llewellyn Worldwide Ltd. cannot guarantee that every letter written to the author can be answered, but all will be forwarded. Please write to:

Atherton Drenth
℅ Llewellyn Worldwide
2143 Wooddale Drive
Woodbury, MN 55125-2989

Please enclose a self-addressed stamped envelope for reply,
or $1.00 to cover costs. If outside the U.S.A., enclose
an international postal reply coupon.

Many of Llewellyn's authors have websites with additional information and resources. For more information, please visit our website at http://www.llewellyn.com

GET MORE AT LLEWELLYN.COM

Visit us online to browse hundreds of our books and decks, plus sign up to receive our e-newsletters and exclusive online offers.

- • Free tarot readings • Spell-a-Day • Moon phases
- • Recipes, spells, and tips • Blogs • Encyclopedia
- • Author interviews, articles, and upcoming events

GET SOCIAL WITH LLEWELLYN

Find us on
Facebook
www.Facebook.com/LlewellynBooks

Follow us on
twitter™
www.Twitter.com/Llewellynbooks

GET BOOKS AT LLEWELLYN

LLEWELLYN ORDERING INFORMATION

Order online: Visit our website at www.llewellyn.com to select your books and place an order on our secure server.

Order by phone:
- • Call toll free within the U.S. at 1-877-NEW-WRLD (1-877-639-9753)
- • Call toll free within Canada at 1-866-NEW-WRLD (1-866-639-9753)
- • We accept VISA, MasterCard, American Express and Discover

Order by mail:
Send the full price of your order (MN residents add 6.875% sales tax) in U.S. funds, plus postage and handling to: Llewellyn Worldwide, 2143 Wooddale Drive Woodbury, MN 55125-2989

POSTAGE AND HANDLING

STANDARD (U.S. & Canada):
(Please allow 12 business days)
$30.00 and under, add $4.00.
$30.01 and over, FREE SHIPPING.

INTERNATIONAL ORDERS:
$16.00 for one book, plus $3.00 for each additional book.

Visit us online for more shipping options. Prices subject to change.

FREE CATALOG!

To order, call 1-877-NEW-WRLD ext. 8236 or visit our website

TAMING
THE DRUNKEN
MONKEY

The Path to Mindfulness, Meditation, and Increased Concentration

WILLIAM L. MIKULAS, PhD

Taming the Drunken Monkey
The Path to Mindfulness, Meditation, and Increased Concentration
William L. Mikulas PhD

The mind often behaves like a drunken monkey—largely out of control. Instead of falling victim to stress, anxiety, and frustration, learn how to tame your consciousness with this easy-to-follow guide to mindfulness. With thorough mental training that moves beyond the basics, you'll effectively enhance the health of your body, mind, and spirit.

Drawing from Western and Eastern psychologies, health systems, and wisdom traditions, *Taming the Drunken Monkey* provides a reader-friendly system that progresses steadily through the five levels of study, from novice to master. Develop and improve the three basic behaviors of the mind: concentration, awareness, and mental flexibility. Discover the power of breathwork with yogic pranayama, Chinese medicine, and Western respiratory science. Apply useful exercises and practices to your life based on health, meditation, body awareness, spiritual awakening, and more.

978-0-7387-3469-9, 288 pp., 5 ¼ x 8   **$16.99**

DELLA TEMPLE

Tame Your Inner Critic

Find Peace & Contentment
to Live Your Life
on Purpose

Tame Your Inner Critic
Find Peace & Contentment to Live Your Life on Purpose
DELLA TEMPLE

Uncover the authentic you, control the critic within, and find the peace you need to live your life on purpose. Learn to silence the persistent chatter of your inner critic and replace it with the voice of your inner guidance—your spirit.

Tame Your Inner Critic takes you on a journey of self-discovery, exploring the energy of your thoughts and turning the negative into positive. Discover how to use your innate intuitive abilities to heal these energies and discard judgments and criticisms that have built up over the years. Find your true north—your own internal wisdom that is connected to the divine and gives you guidance. With specialized exercises and meditations, this book shows you how to banish negativity, improve your relationships, and realize new ways to share your gifts with the world around you.

978-0-7387-4395-0, 264 pp., 5 ¼ x 8   **$15.99**

THE MINDFULNESS HABIT

**Six Weeks to Creating
the Habit of Being Present**

KATE SCIANDRA

The Mindfulness Habit
Six Weeks to Creating the Habit of Being Present
Kate Sciandra

This step-by-step book offers a de-mystified and non-time-consuming approach to being present. It addresses the difference between meditation and mindfulness, why mindfulness is important, and dispels common misconceptions about the process. It then takes a step-by-step approach to not only teach exercises and techniques for developing mindfulness, but also includes instructions for finding the everyday opportunities to put them in place. This is done in a way that uses habit-forming principles so that at the end of six weeks, you have both a tool kit and a habit for using it regularly.

The Mindfulness Habit helps you understand the value of living in the moment and offers many ways to create the habit of finding opportunities for mindfulness. In each section of the book, you'll discover information about a variety of topics, exercises and instructions for building mindful habits in your life, and much more.

978-0-7387-4189-5, 216 pp., 5 x 7   **$16.99**

Robert
Butera PhD   Erin
Byron MA   Staffan
Elgelid PhD, P.T.

yoga
therapy
for
stress &
anxiety

Create a Personalized Holistic Plan to Balance Your Life

Yoga Therapy for Stress and Anxiety
Create a Personalized Holistic Plan to Balance Your Life
Robert Butera PhD
Erin Byron MA
Staffan Elgelid PhD, P.T.

Create a personalized path to healing with this step-by-step guide to holistic change. Comprehensive and accessible no matter your skill level, *Yoga Therapy for Stress and Anxiety* helps you understand what creates a stress-filled life so that you may choose a life of ease instead. Through yoga practice and the lesser-known lifestyle aspects of yoga, you will be able to face all situations from the calm perspective of the higher self.

Incorporating exercises, breathing techniques, meditation, and many other tools, this guide provides effective methods for repairing areas of imbalance and identifying your needs. Learn about the five yogic paths of psychology, intellect, health, work, and relationships. Apply a variety of yoga postures for relaxation, improved attitude and sleep, self-acceptance, and more. With the transformative power of a whole-lifestyle approach, you will achieve wellness in your mind, body, and soul.

978-0-7387-4575-6, 360 pp., 6 x 9   **$19.99**

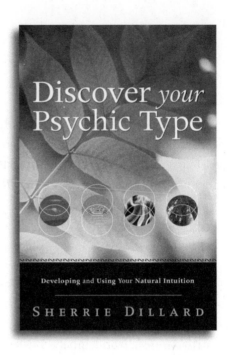

Discover *your* **Psychic Type**

Developing and Using Your Natural Intuition

S H E R R I E   D I L L A R D

Discover Your Psychic Type
Developing and Using Your Natural Intuition
SHERRIE DILLARD

Intuition and spiritual growth are indelibly linked, according to professional psychic and therapist Sherrie Dillard. Offering a personalized approach to psychic development, this breakthrough guide introduces four different psychic types and explains how to develop the unique spiritual capabilities of each.

Are you a physical, mental, emotional, or spiritual intuitive? Take Dillard's insightful quiz to find out. Discover more about each type's intuitive nature, personality, potential physical weaknesses, and more. There are guided meditations for each kind of intuitive, as well as exercises to hone your psychic skills. Remarkable stories from the author's professional life illustrate the incredible power of intuition and its connection to the spirit world, inner wisdom, and your higher self.

From psychic protection to spirit guides to mystical states, Dillard offers guidance as you evolve toward the final destination of every psychic type: union with the divine.

978-0-7387-1278-9, 288 pp., 5 ¼ x 8   **$15.99**

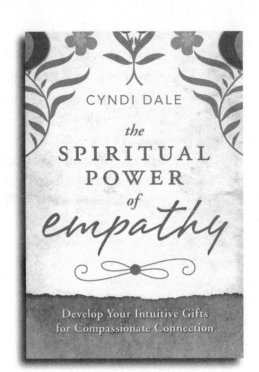

CYNDI DALE

the

SPIRITUAL
POWER

of

empathy

Develop Your Intuitive Gifts
for Compassionate Connection

The Spiritual Power of Empathy
Develop Your Intuitive Gifts for Compassionate Connection
Cyndi Dale

For some, the empathic gift provides insight and inspiration, but for others, empathy creates feelings of confusion and panic. *The Spiritual Power of Empathy* is a hands-on training course for empaths, showing you how to comfortably use this often-unrecognized ability for better relationships, career advancement, raising children, and healing the self and others.

Join popular author Cyndi Dale as she shares ways to develop the six empathic types, techniques for screening and filtering information, and tips for opening up to a new world of deeper connections with the loved ones in your life. Also includes important information for dealing with the difficulties empaths often face, such as being overwhelmed in a crowd.

978-0-7387-3799-7, 264 pp., 6 x 9   **$16.99**

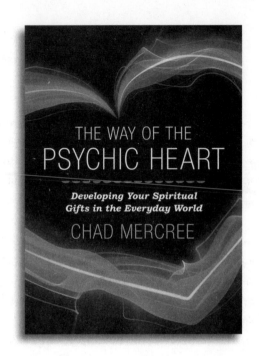

The Way of the Psychic Heart
Developing Your Spiritual Gifts in the Everyday World
Chad Mercree

Developing your natural psychic abilities begins with an open heart, and the more you connect with your heart, the easier your psychic abilities flow. In this introduction to psychic development, learning to embrace your spiritual gifts is based on the three pillars: developing awareness, auric vision, and intuition.

The Way of the Psychic Heart is a four-part, easy-to-use guide about embarking on your own spiritual path. Everyone is psychic; it's a normal state that we've forgotten and must get back in touch with through the heart, rather than learning and practicing just from the mind. Reconnect with your psychic heart through quizzes, question prompts, exercises, personal stories from the author, and simple instruction. With practice and the keys to develop your abilities presented in this book, you'll integrate intuition into everything you do.

978-0-7387-4040-9, 336 pp., 5 x 7   **$15.99**

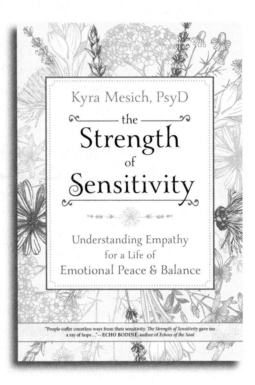

Kyra Mesich, PsyD

the

Strength

of

Sensitivity

Understanding Empathy
for a Life of
Emotional Peace & Balance

"People suffer countless ways from their sensitivity. *The Strength of Sensitivity* gave me
a ray of hope…"—ECHO BODINE, author of *Echoes of the Soul*

The Strength of Sensitivity
Understanding Empathy for a Life of Emotional Peace & Balance
Kyra Mesich PsyD

Empathic ability is a profound reminder that we are all connected. However, it's not always easy to cope with. For highly sensitive people, it can feel like an invasion, leading to confusion, physical issues, depression, and emotional distress.

The Strength of Sensitivity explores the causes of empathic and psychic connections, providing techniques for developing and coping with sensitivity in a positive way. Join author Kyra Mesich, PsyD, as she shares stories about the struggles and triumphs of being an empath while sharing amazing scientific research that explains how this connection works. Discover tools such as flower essences, meditation, and a twenty-day, four-step practice that effectively help sensitive people create healthier relationships with their empathic abilities. Holistic psychology has shed new light on sensitivity; let this guide show you how to live intuitively every day while integrating your whole body, mind, and spirit.

978-0-7387-4849-8, 216 pp., 6 x 9 $16.99
